County Tales

Facts, Legends and Yarns of Northamptonshire

Alan Burman

Produced and Published by
Jones-Sands Publishing
Coventry England

Credits for photographs and illustrations.
The photographs and illustrations throughout this book
are from the Alan Burman Collection.

Copyright © 1992 by Jones-Sands Publishing

Printed in the United Kingdom

ISBN 0 947764 31 9

All rights reserved. No part of this publication other than short extracts for review purposes may be reproduced, stored in a retrieval system, or transmitted, in any form or by any means, electronic, photocopying, recording or otherwise without the express permission of the publishers.

Conditions of sale. This book is sold subject to the condition that it shall not, by way of trade or otherwise, be lent, re-sold, hired out or otherwise circulated without the publishers prior consent in any form of binding or cover other than that in which it is published and without a similar condition including this condition being imposed on the subsequent purchaser.

For a full list of Jones-Sands Publications, especially those based on Northampton and Northamptonshire, please write or telephone Jones Sands Publishing, 10 Startin Close, Exhall, Coventry CV7 9NA. Telephone: (0203)365640.

CONTENTS

Coaching Days On Northamptonshire's Roads 1
A Walk Through Goff's Field 9
A Tale Of A Skirt 13
Rinking Through The Years 17
Where Priests Hid For Their Lives 21
Music Hall Lived On In Clubs 29
From Beyond The Grave.... 33
Abington's Pierrots 35
Northampton's Horse Racing Course 39
Carthorse Wins The Grand National 43
Northampton's Royal Park 45
The Great School War 49
A Can-Tank-Erous Tale 53
A Macabre Murder At Guilsborough 57
Jumbo Skulls At Cotton End 61
St. James's Abbey 63
The Boy O'Bell Barn 69
Some County Characters 71
The Kingsthorpe Coal Mine 75
Sweet Adeline Of Deene 79
Battle Of The River Nene 85
Doing The Northampton Canter.... 87
Magic .... And .... Tragic .... Gates 89
Ridicule In Camera 91
The King's Artificial Limb.... 95
How Paddy's Meadow Got It's Name 97
Parachute Joe 99
The Galloping Ghost Of Sywell 101
The Decline And Fall Of Northampton's Castle 103

FOREWORD

As Editor of the Chronicle and Echo in 1985, I can claim some responsibility for the launch of the weekly series of articles *Alan Burman's County Tales*. I was particularly pleased, therefore to be asked to write a foreword for this compilation.

I recall my very first assignment for the Chronicle and Echo as a naive but enthusiastic young trainee reporter, in 1959. It was to interview a couple celebrating their golden wedding, and Alan accompanied me to take their photograph.

I thought I had the story pretty well covered, and the aged pair went off to fetch us the regulation cup of tea. "When they come back I'll quiz them, you just get it all down," said Alan. He then proceeded to extract from the couple the extraordinary and amusing account of their 50 years together which had me scribbling away for half-an-hour or more. The Editor was well pleased with the piece - all thanks to Alan.

The details of the story are lost to me now, but I wouldn't be surprised if they were filed away somewhere, ready to appear as a future County Tale.

As long as I have known him Alan has had a rare appreciation of the unusual, and of the past, not in the sense of dull history but in anecdotal glimpses of some small aspect of it and the fascinating, sometimes eccentric, characters who were part of it.

This book is a result of that love of the odd aspects of life in years gone by - and Northamptonshire certainly seems to be a rich source.

Phil Green

INTRODUCTION

Let me say, right from the start, that I am no historian. I am, however, hooked on history.

County Tales series of articles, which first appeared in the Chronicle & Echo newspaper in September 1985 and have been a regular weekly feature ever since, were conceived over a pint in a pub.

Four pals and I would go for a drink each Thursday night, taking it in turns to drive. It became a point of honour to visit a different village inn each week. Quaffing ale, we would dredge some tale concerning the area from the dark recesses of our memories and retell it. Locals frequently capped our anecdotes with other yarns, and so the store of odd facts grew. After a while, one of my friends said, "You ought to write these stories down, you know". That's how County Tales came about.

They are called Tales because I do not claim that they are the definitive history of any particular subject, but the essential facts in a readable and digestible form. I had enough of dry history at school! Anyway, I did not want to be restricted from recounting legend, historical hearsay, or even contemporary gossip by calling them anything else but tales.

Proper historians may charge that my tales lack depth and analysis. I can only plead guilty and offer the excuse that, when writing to fill a particular space in the layout of a newspaper, the problem generally is, how to shorten the story, rather than how to fill the space, in short, what to leave out. I can only suggest that, if this book whets your appetite for more historical detail, there is a wealth of information to be gathered either at the Central Library Local Studies Room, or at the County Records Office, Wootton Hall. Both of these sources have been of inestimable help to me, over the years, and I acknowledge this with thanks.

The great thing about local history is that it enables you to travel the county and, no matter how badly the area has been desecrated by developers, you can say to yourself, "So and so happened there", or, "Such and such a building once stood there", and imagine how it once was. It all doesn't seem so bad then.

My aim then is merely to amuse ...... and don't let anyone tell you differently, history is fun!

Coaching Days On Northamptonshire's Roads

In the golden age of coaching Northamptonshire was the crossroads of England. The country was criss-crossed with stage and mail coach routes, many of which passed through the county.

The busiest road in the country was the Holyhead Road, 23 miles of which was in Northamptonshire, following either the line of the old Watling Street or diverging west at Weedon to head for Coventry. Other routes both north/south and east/west passed through Northampton itself like the spokes of a wheel. This county's roads were infamous for their heavy clay and so, in the 17th century, everyone who could travelled on horseback.

A posthorse system was established in 1635 by the Post Office, letters being charged for at 2½d per mile. Changing horses along the way, the journey from London to Holyhead took 6 days. Just five years later the first ever stage coach was introduced to England. By 1657 a regular stage coach service was operating on the Holyhead Road, leaving the George Inn, Aldersgate, in London for Chester three times a week. Its journey up through Stony Stratford and Towcester to Coventry took two days and cost each traveller 25/-, the trip to Chester taking four days and costing 35/-.

The establishment of turnpikes put the onus of road improvements on the trustees, and the better surfaces encouraged the development of faster, more comfortable coaches. The entire section of road between Hockliffe and Dunchurch was turnpike as were other routes through the county. A small six-sided tollhouse stood by the gate at Cock Lane, Kingsthorpe, and controlled the roads to Harborough and Welford. The fees charged paid for the roads to be made up and metalled.

John Palmer, a theatre proprietor of Bath, had the idea of establishing a network of coaches to carry mail and on 2nd August 1784 the first ever mail coach ran between London and Bath covering the 115 miles in 17 hours. Just one year later the first mailcoach ran through Northampton. It ran to Holyhead by a 278 mile roundabout route via Welford, Lutterworth and Chester. Soon the mail coach was king of the road. All other traffic was obliged to give way to it, it paid no tolls, and was often the fastest vehicle on the highway. By 1797 there were 42 mail coaches operating through Towcester on the Watling Street alone, not to mention the many running from Oxford and Northampton. Letters were

Coaching Days on Northamptonshire's Roads

A coach leaving Northampton via the Kingsthorpe turnpike. The six sided tollhouse and its tollgate can be seen in the distance, at the top of Cock Lane, close by the Cock Inn.

charged, on delivery, at 4d for 15 miles and 1/5d for 70 miles.

As travel moved into the 19th century a golden age of coaching dawned. The new "parliamentary" route to Holyhead was opened in 1817, the route leaving the old Watling Street at Weedon Bec and heading off for Coventry, rejoining the old route 73 miles further on. This became known as the New Holyhead Mail route, and covered 260 miles, while the old way was called the Holyhead and Chester Mail. The H & C coach left the Swan with Two Necks in Lad Lane at 7.30 pm each night taking 38 hours to cover the 278 miles. When the Menai Bridge was opened in 1826 the time went down to 32¾ hours while, four years later, the time was reduced again to 29 hours 17 minutes.

The roads, by now, were thronged with crack stage coaches and mails whose names were as well-known to travellers then as the Flying Scot and Concorde is today. Some ran whole routes, never dropping below 12 miles per hour and hitting a full 18¾ mph on good stretches, and were precisely timed to the minute. The Red Rover and the Beehive went through Towcester on their way to Birmingham and Manchester. The Crown Prince went via Towcester to Daventry and Southam. Through Daventry went the Royal Mail, the Standard, the Express and the Albion, the latter on its way to Liverpool. Northampton itself originated several routes as well as being the calling point on many others. The Northampton ran to London from the Dolphin Inn, while the Reindeer operated to Oxford. The Sovereign connected Northampton with Liverpool.

Others leaving Northampton rejoiced in names like the Independent, the Royal Mail, the Regulator, the Royal Bruce, the Telegraph, the Royal Defiance, the Rocket, the Eagle, the Lark and the Umpire. The Express and the Courier came to Northampton from London via Newport Pagnell and went on to Leeds, while the Hope went to Sheffield.

Through Kettering went the romantically named Peveril of the Peak, which originally travelled to Manchester via Dunstable and Northampton, but later changed its route to serve Bedford. In 1831 its proprietor William Gilbert extended the route to Edinburgh, arriving there 44 hours after leaving London.

At the peak of the coaching age 700 Royal Mail coaches operated in England. The nightly departure of many of these from the G.P.O. headquarters at St. Martin le Grand, in London, was considered a great spectacle, with the colourful coaches, the cries of coachmen and the many different tunes being played by the guards on the coach-horns, the so-called "yard of tin".

All horsing of these coaches was by contract and it was big business. One operator William Chapman owned 3,000 coaches and 150,000 horses. He employed 30,000 drivers, guards and ostlers and ran 27 mail coaches out of London every night. The mail coaches were in the charge of the guard, who was a Post Office employee, and he was empowered to control, and indeed fine for lateness, the driver. At ½ guinea a week retainer and an annual suit of clothes they were badly paid for the job, which was cold, wet and exhausting, particularly in the depths of a bad winter, and they were expected to make up a decent wage from tips. Passengers would be prompted by the utterance "I leaves yer 'ere, gentlemen", and a poor response, or a tiny tip, would be met with heavy sarcasm. This was known as "kicking the passengers". The coachman, himself, was employed by the contractor and was usually paid by distance, typical being Chapmans rate of 2/- for 50 miles, a busy driver, if he was lucky, making some £400 a year.

Drivers of mail and crack stage coaches became famous figures with their own fan following. Samuel Inns of Towcester was one celebrated whip whose patronage by the gentry allowed him to retire as a prosperous farmer. William Chapman's famous coachman was Joseph Pearson who drove the routes north from Northampton. After many years without an accident, he was killed in a coaching accident whilst riding as a passenger. Another famous coachman was Mat Seyzinger, a Northampton man. He was coachman on the Nottingham Times, while his guard was another local man, Bill Wright. Seyzinger is buried in All Saints churchyard. These ace coachmen were known to race, too, although strict rules, particularly for mail coaches, forbade it. On May Day 1830 the Independent Tally Ho leaving London for Birmingham raced to put up a new record time for the 109 mile run. It covered the journey in 7 hours 39 minutes including all horse changes.

Young bloods, kitted out in stylish versions of the coachman's wear and using the best quality whips made at Daventry, the famous centre of the whipmakers craft, who aspired to becoming experts "with the ribbons" competed to occupy the box beside the ace drivers. Though it was not strictly allowed, a bribe could sometimes persuade the coachman to hand over the reins of a crack coach, and then things speeded up as the coach was raced as fast as the horses would go.

The horses, on all but the crack coaches, were often poor old nags. Indeed, coachmen referred to all horses as cattle. Quality "wheelers" could be used to mask other bad horses. Chapmans, one of the better outfits, bought high quality leaders at £17 each and wheelers at £25 each, though, more commonly, ex carriage-horses either with bad habits or temperaments, or nearing the end of their working lives were "used up" in coach service. Coachmen did not favour horses marked with "socks". There was an old saying:-

One white leg, buy him,
Two white legs, try him,
Three white legs, look about him,
Four white legs, go without him.

The drivers raced to reach the busy stables first, as the first coaches often got the best horses. For this reason many accidents happened running down the hills north and south of Towcester.

The winter was a hard time for coachmen. Their many-layered, heavy coats would get soaked and often froze into solid ice. The familiar Christmas card scene of the coach stuck in the snow was all too common. In January and February of 1799 the country was paralysed by deep snow and blizzards. Most routes were affected and many coaches abandoned in drifts, some still being missing at the end of April. Again, on Christmas Day 1836, snow brought the country to a halt. There were 40 foot drifts in places. The Leeds Mail heading for Northampton from Melton Mowbray was lost for days and 17 coaches were embedded in drifts between Coventry and Northampton. The Watling Street was littered with abandoned coaches. Under these circumstances it was the guard's duty, on mail coaches, to take one of the horses and ride on with the post, leaving the coachman and passengers to fend for themselves.

Other hazards afflicted the unfortunate travellers, too, not least of which was the risk of accident. Just north of Towcester, at the quaintly named Dirt House Hill, a bad smash occurred on 29th June 1838. The Holyhead Mail had left Birmingham the day before, which happened to be Queen Victoria's Coronation Day. Amid the crowds and excitement the guard had failed to check the lamps, which were later found to be missing. Ascending the hill in the northbound direction was the Carlisle Mail, which had just left Towcester, and coming up fast behind was the crack Manchester Mail. Loath to lose speed on the hill, the Manchester Mail overtook the Carlisle coach. While on the wrong side of the road the unlit Holyhead Mail came over the brow and collided head on. Many horses were killed and injured, and passengers maimed. The fact that the harness was found to be old and brittle and had snapped upon impact was said to have reduced the injuries.

A year earlier the Emerald coach, on its way from London to Birmingham had an axletree break at 2 am in the morning, overturning the coach outside Little Brickhill. The five passengers riding outside were thrown safely into the hedge, but John Webb, the unfortunate coachman, got tangled up with the apron and was crushed to death under the vehicle. Just outside Towcester, near Cuttle Mill, where the road ran along an embankment, the Emerald coach again crashed in August 1837. This time the horses bolted over the hill, upsetting the coach in the dip beyond. The outside passengers were thrown over twenty feet and two of them were killed.

In Northampton itself Jem Welby, an old local coachman, overturned a coach in the town. When asked to explain it, he said that he had tipped the passengers out to count them......

Then there was the further danger of robbery. Highwaymen and robbers were not the gentlemen of the road as romantically depicted, but were more often thugs and murderers. In 1784 the Northampton bound coach was held up by two "well horsed thieves wearing plain

Coaching Days on Northamptonshire's Roads

A stagecoach passes All Saints in the 1830s, during the heyday of coaching.

clothes" who stole a gold enamelled French watch in a black sealskin case. A guinea reward was offered. Earlier, on 12th September, 1732, three highwaymen were operating at Hackleton. By the crossroads there two of them held up the Nottingham and the Northampton stagecoaches while the third kept lookout. They took £100 in cash, a portmanteau and a cloak bag. Some of the contents were found, discarded, at Queen Eleanors Cross, which suggests that the robbers were town men.

A daring robbery of a different kind happened on the Watling Street in March 1835. Four men booked inside seats on the Greyhound coach out of London. Two left the coach at Hockcliffe and the other two at Stony Stratford. Soon after, the guard had occasion to open up the luggage locker, when he found that the contents had been removed by cutting in from the passenger compartment. Three hundred gold sovereigns and a £120 bank draft were taken.

Even hi-jacking was not unknown. The Eclipse coach, one November day in 1829, was on its way from Birmingham via Towcester to London. Aboard were 3 officers from Chester gaol and 12 convicts due to be transported to Botany Bay, chained in pairs. They had all already been involved in one coach accident, when the Albion had crashed at Walsall. In the confusion one prisoner had stolen the master key. After being housed overnight in Moor Street Prison they were now entering Northamptonshire. Near Dunchurch they overpowered the guards, unlocked their fetters, and galloped off across country on the coach horses. Two were never seen again.

Coach travellers were accustomed to the grisly sight of the bodies of criminals hanging by the wayside, the gibbets and gallows being intended as a dire warning. On the Watling Street fifteen miles north of Weedon, where the A426 now crosses the road, the junction is still called Gibbet Hill. In years gone by it was known as Loseby Gibbet, set up in 1687 and named after the first murderer hung upon it. The landmark was shown on the meticulous timetables of the coaches. The gallows on the edge of Northampton, near today's White Elephant pub, saw Thomas Brown on 28th March 1794 and William James (alias Johns) with John Taylor in March 1801, hanged for highway robbery.

Graves, too, littered the coach roads, for suicides were refused burial in most churchyards, and so were frequently interred, superstitiously, at crossroads. As coaching's golden age came to a close, with the railways capturing most of the business with their superior speed and comfort, coaches had reached a high state of organisation and speed. In 1838 a horse rider named Samuel Daniels raced against the Telegraph coach from London to Northampton for a wager, and only beat it by one and a half minutes......

As the coach network withered and died, the proprietors were not the only ones to suffer. Inns and stables had to cut back or find new business. In Northampton the Cock Inn at Kingsthorpe, the calling place of the famous Manchester Telegraph, was hit, as was the Angel Inn, the town's principal coaching inn kept by landlord Thomas Shaw, himself one of the largest coach proprietors outside of London.

In the last two years of service the Holyhead Mail did the trip from London to Holyhead in 26 hours 55 minutes. The coach which left London at 8 pm arrived at Towcester at 2.12 am or Daventry at 3.25 am. In 1839 the last coach left London for Birmingham on the famous Holyhead Road. Some rural routes, particularly across country, survived briefly, but, on 6th January 1846 the very last mail coach arrived at London from Norwich and Newmarket, and sounded the deathknell of the coaching age.

In 1857 the 8th Duke of Beaufort and a number of other rich enthusiasts, recalling the great days of the mail coach parades, the last of which had been held in 1838, decided

The Times coach with the team pulling hard at Ascot race meeting.

to set up a club to preserve and encourage the art of driving, and so set up the Four in Hand Club. Just a few years later, in 1871, the rival Coaching Club was started. These clubs were instrumental in saving a great number of the old coaches which were mouldering in yards all over the country. In 1874, for instance, at a joint meeting of the two clubs coinciding with the Ascot race meeting, 122 coaches turned up.

A Northampton man, Mr. Robert Frisby became a stalwart of these clubs and ran coaches of all sorts right up until the second World War. He ran the Times mail coach, and others, for many years, in 1907 putting up a record drive from Northampton to London in 9½ hours. That same year he came fourth in the Coaching Marathon against many American millionaire enthusiasts. Sadly, they were disposed of, one being sold to Bertram Mills Circus, another going, via a dealer at Peterborough, to Chessington Zoo. Another was eventually sold in 1939 for £5 to be broken up, the last four in hand to work out of the town.

So ended the history of coaching in Northampton, when its importance as the hub of England diminished. Now the town is growing in stature for the same reasons, as a superb distribution point and junction for travellers.

Mr. Robert Frisby and his Times coach drawn up outside the Peacock Hotel on the Market Square prior to taking a load of passengers to Towcester Races.

A Walk Through Goff's Field

With the evenings lengthening and springtime upon us I recall a regular countryside walk of my childhood. I lived in Seymour Street, St. James's End, and on spring or summer nights would walk with my parents to Old Duston, where we would refresh ourselves at a village pub before returning home at dusk.

Most of the route was by hedgerows and fields in areas now obliterated by industrial development, but let's relive the past awhile.

As we crossed Spencer Bridge Road the rooks were creating a racket in the two giant elms on the Green. These trees had been there before the houses round about were built, and survived upon the insistence of Earl Spencer, who had the plans altered especially to preserve them. The rooks had first nested here in 1909 and several generations of Jimmy's Enders grew up with the country sound of cawing birds outside their windows.

Passing the narrow passage of the outdoor beer house at the end of Aberdeen Terrace, we enter the Scottish Streets. My mother would tell me of the soldiers of the Highland regiments who were billeted in the town during the First World War parading with their pipers through these streets with Scottish place names. Curiously, they are laid out in alphabetical order, Argyle Street, Bruce Street, C is missed, Dundee Street, Elgin Street, Forfar Street, Glasgow Street, and Holyrood Road. There had once, apparently, been a Coupar Street but it caused confusion with Cowper Street in another part of the town, so was renamed Fyfe Street.

Sounds of laughter and cheerful shouts came over the wall from Franklin's Gardens, by Melbourne Terrace, for on the other side was the popular swimming pool with its large cascade. The screech of the many peacocks that roamed the Gardens echoed among the avenues of limes, too, mixed with the country sounds of other animals. The licensee, former Saints player Jerry Gordon, had rabbits (at one time as many as 700), ponies, horses, hens, ducks, geese, 20 pigs, goats and bees!.

Just beyond, we passed the Red House public house, now the Red Rover, where families sat in the extensive gardens at the rear.

This looked out on to fields that stretched beyond to Bants Lane. The Malcolm Drive estate was yet to be built, with bungalows costing £465.....! Opposite was Mr. Halls greengrocer shop. Most of his business, in fact, was done from a handcart which he pushed around the End, not along the streets, but back and forth along the "jitties", shouting his wares and selling the produce.

As we reached the junction where the Duston Road left the Weedon Road we could look into the gardens of the luxurious houses there. The Limes always interested me as it was owned by the Grose family and there was often an unusual high quality motor-car parked in the drive. From this point one could look back and see the clock of St. James's Church. The tower was built, I was told, as a memorial by the Grose's after the first war and arranged so that it was visible from their family home.

Now we began to enter countryside proper, hedgerows lining the road. On the south side tall hawthorn gave way, briefly, to a short row of villas, not much more than half a dozen. This was the very edge of town, I always thought. Alongside the last house ran a narrow footpath. Little more than a shoulder's width, it was a green chasm between two tall, thick hedges, hedges that were home to all sorts of birds, whose nests we searched for. I was allowed to cup the warm, delicately mottled eggs in the palm of my hands before they were returned to the nest by my father.

Suddenly the path opened out into Goff's Field. An ancient meadow, in springtime it was almost waist deep in buttercups and daisies; at least, up to my child-height waist. After wading through these flowers I would emerge with my woollen socks and short grey flannel trousers dusted yellow with pollen. On the wet bottom of the field grew huge waxen-flowered molly-blobs, while at the headland bloomed tall moon-daisies. The hedgerows sprouted pale green in the spring and we ate "bread and cheese", the edible shoots of the hawthorn. Soon all of this turned to snowy white with may-blossom. The smell of this is an abiding memory of spring for me, for, though we often gathered may-blossom and brought it home it was never allowed into the house, it being considered very unlucky to do so. Here and there in the hedgerows were crab-apples and sloes punctuating the may with pink blossom tints. Later, in the autumn, we would return for the fruits.

Walking the top of the field we would skirt the churchyard wall of St. Luke's, Duston's parish church. Visible from the field was a tomb which fascinated this child. Presumably the resting place of a seafaring man, it had on it's top an anchor embedded in the stone.

Two gates now brought us to Mill Lane where, if we looked right before crossing, we could see two old thatched cottages and frequently encountered some amateur artist picturing the scene. We, however went straight across the lane, by the front of a large detached Victorian house to turn right into another narrow footpath. This one was bounded on the left by a field which always seemed to hold horses. A meagre hedge restrained them from entering the path though their seemingly huge heads often scared me stiff as they investigated our passing. On the right was the wall of the garden and in this was a gate. Sometimes this would carry a handwritten notice offering fruit for sale. I would sometimes be sent here to buy some for jam making and be taken to the potting shed by a grizzled old gardener where, in aromatic mustiness, he would fill my basket with plums, pears or apples. In my mind's eye the whole scene has an uncanny resemblance to the faded prints that my grandmother was so fond of.

So we went on, to emerge in Melbourne Lane. Diagonally left was the Melbourne

Arms pub. Named after Lord Melbourne, one-time Prime Minister, who owned estates hereabouts, it was an unusual pub in that it had gardens on the opposite side of the road.

The gardens had, at their top end, an open fronted shelter overgrown with ivy and lilac. The rear of this was a jungle of tangled shrubbery, a great playground for us children. Bullocks in the field beyond had learned long ago that easy pickings could be had in the form of crisps and crackers, so they often lined the fence looking for titbits. The lane outside was busy with men and waiters crossing the road with trays of drinks, though to no-ones danger, as this was a cul-de-sac leading only to Berrywood fields.

At the end of the evening, tired out, I would return home on the shoulders of my father, usually by a different route. Perhaps we would go through Duston village, emerging into the countryside by the vicarage. British Timken, of course, had not invaded the area by then. We would bear left into Bants Lane where, from the Duston end, we could look across the dip in the lane towards Dallington. On both sides were fields where, in later years, I roamed freely with other urchins. In the hollow were clustered the red-brick buildings of a farm.

Thus on towards Harlestone Road and the crossroads at Dallington Park. From here, if we looked left, we could see in the distance the wooden "Dr. Who"-type police box and beyond it the dark clump of the "flea tree". This was an overgrown blackthorn, thick and matted as the hair of the tramps who gathered in it's shelter for a brew-up before walking the three miles in to the workhouse.

Soon after passing Dallington Park we would pause at a deep bank in the shade of four large trees at the rear of Spencer School. This small area was thick with scented violets in the spring and many locals gathered posies here. Past the gates of the ugly redbrick vicarage where, sometimes, the bespectacled Rev. Robinson could be seen, and on to home.

Now, unfortunately, the whole of this walk is covered with industry and development. Brick and concrete have obliterated the meadows and hedgerows, but the mind is a wonderful thing, retaining pictures and senses of long ago for "replay" at will. So, in my head at least, this idyll lives on.

A Tale of a Skirt

A fashionable craze led to a strange strike in Northampton's clothing industry in 1911. The fuss was all over the hobble skirt.

The hobble skirt, like so many of the more ridiculous of womens fashions, was taken to extremes. The tight, clinging skirt so restricted leg movement that the wearer could only take tiny steps and was effectively hobbled. The more fashionable women also competed to wear as little as possible beneath the ankle-length garment, and it was this which sparked off the strike.

At the Brook Manufacturing Company's premises in Clarke Road 1,200 girls were employed, chiefly in the making of the flouncy, lace-trimmed, petticoats that had sold so well for years. Until the coming of the hobble, that is, when the trade "was crippled like the steps of the wearers of this fashion". Demand for such lingerie dropped dramatically.

Rather than dismiss any of the girls, the younger ones, some only 13 years of age, were put to work machining pinafores for 5d (2p) per dozen. The girls said that they could only earn 6/6d per week at this rate, while the firm asserted that they could earn between 12/- and 15/- and that this was better than nothing during a slack period.

One Friday morning in October 1911, 120 of the machinists came out on strike without warning, parading the street and singing slogans. Next day more women joined the protest bringing the numbers up to 200.

On Monday morning the company struck back. All 1,200 workers arrived at the factory to find the doors locked and bolted. It was a lockout. With the prospect of a wageless week ahead, some of the women faced extreme hardship, and the firm relented to the extent that they decided to hold stocktaking early, employing some of the women on the task. Union leaders, however, quickly stepped in to ban the move.

Though none of the strikers were union members, a lady organiser of the newly formed National Federation of Women Workers, a Mrs. Lowen, arrived from London and initially arranged a mass meeting at the Trade Hall on Monday afternoon. 500 women packed like sardines into the hall which normally accommodated 300, where they chanted "war songs" and cheered their leaders. One song went:-

> *We won't do pinafores,*
> *We won't do pinafores.*
> *But the Brook their fortunes made.*
> *What we want are white skirts*
> *They're in better form.*
> *So shout out together girls,*
> *We won't do pinafores!*

The platform was lined with local socialists, councillors, and sympathisers. Councillor Pitt said that he had heard of one young girl whose parents had threatened to throw her out on the street if she went on strike, and he appealed to older workers to support their young sisters. Mrs. Lowen, though a "slim and delicate looking figure", delivered a fiery speech. "I don't care if I have to face one boss, or two, or a dozen", she said, " I am ready to face them all on one condition only. When they ask me how many girls I represent, I want to say one word and one word only" .... "ALL", bellowed the girls. "Are you willing to be Federated?", she asked ...... "YES", they replied.

She then claimed that for every 7/- that the workers earned the firm got £1. This was enough for the workers, and there and then it was resolved to set up a local branch of the National Federation of Women Workers, electing officers on the spot. Next morning a conference was held between Mrs. Lowen and three of the Brook's partners. Outside an excited throng of girls was kept in order by two burly constables. Kate Goodridge, a young machinist, earned a rousing cheer when she grabbed the horse's head of a delivery cart and led it away down the street after it had tried to enter the factory.

The meeting was held in the sample room of the factory, surrounded by fashionable gowns, robes and blouses. Among the demands made by Mrs. Lowen were that pay rises of between 2d and 6d per dozen should be made for the more difficult work like shirt blouses, and that girls arriving late for work should only be shut out for half an hour, instead of the half day that was then customary. The proprietors, for their part, first insisted that she withdraw the claim that the firm made £1 to every 7/- earned by the workers. If this were so, they said, their profits would be £100,000 per year. Mrs. Lowen withdrew the claim and was told that, in fact, the weekly wage bill was £750.

The firm then offered not to make any worker make pinafores if they preferred not to, letting them remain idle instead. They said that a learner of 13 was given 4/6d per week during training, when they spoiled a lot of work, but that within three months they were earning 10/- to 12/6d per week, although some women who had joined the strike were earning a full £1 a week. The partners asked that,

A cartoon published in the local paper during the strike.

Girl strikers mass outside the Brook Manufacturing Co.'s factory.

during negotiations, sample hands should return to work as the firm was losing valuable orders, including one for 24,000 of one robe alone. Mrs. Lowen effectively, though in a very ladylike way, said "tough luck!"

That night another meeting was called, this time in the Town Hall, where the girls were exhorted to stand firm despite the fact that a rival meeting of 500 contented machinists had earlier gathered in Abington Park and stated their readiness to return to work. One day a pair of terrified Gas Company fitters, arriving at the factory to attend to the gas lamps, fled from a mob of rampaging girls to seek protection behind six police constables. A battle also took place between female strikers and contented workers involving much tearing of hair and scratching.

On Friday evening the strike was finally settled, all the girls returning to work. Wages were to be:- girls 13 to 14 to get 5/- to 5/6d, 14 to 15 with six months service 5/6d to 6/-, 14 to 15 with 12 months service 6/6d to 7/-, 14 to 15 with 13 months service 7/- to 8/-, age 16 with 2 years service 9/- to 10/-, 17 year olds with 2 years service 11/- to 12/-, and aged 18 with 2 years service 13/- to 14/-. Late workers would only lose half an hour's time. The firm stated, however, that, in future, "all machinists who will not and cannot earn fair wages will be discharged".

The strike was the first outburst of female militancy in Northampton's workforce and perhaps echoed the first stirrings of the suffragette movement which found it's voice, locally, the following year.

Rinking Through The Years

"When falling, do not waste time getting down......fall. Don't give a series of contorting exhibitions. There are no soft spots on the rink, so you need not go round feeling for them. Lady novices should not come dressed to kill. The change in visage when one gets on skates is awful in it's suddenness. Wear veils if possible." This was advice given to the skaters of Northampton during the great roller skating craze in the early years of this century.

The pastime of roller skating took Europe by storm as the 20th century came in, and grew into a mania as the years went by. The magazine Punch caricatured it, comic postcards illustrated it, songs featured it, and Charlie Chaplin had fun with it in his films. It was undeniably romantic, too, gliding around with your girl on your arm, with the everpresent possibility of her falling, quite literally, into your arms. The popularity of rinking was thus assured.

By 1909 rinks were being opened in all the large towns, and Northampton was no different. Three such facilities were planned in the town, the American Rink, the George Rink, and the Castle Rink.

The American Roller Rink was the largest of them with a skating area of 200 feet by 70 feet, and was built at the corner of Wellingborough Road and Ardington Road, opposite the Abington Park Hotel. The operating company was headed by Mr. Fred Anderson the proprietor of the Palace Theatre in Gold Street, while the managing director was Mr. George Parkinson who had already opened rinks in Portsmouth, Hull, Huddersfield, Cleethorpes, Halifax, Keighley, and Whitly Bay. The rink surface was of maple laid over a wooden floor with felt in between to give resilience. It had a promenade around it with a gallery for the orchestra.

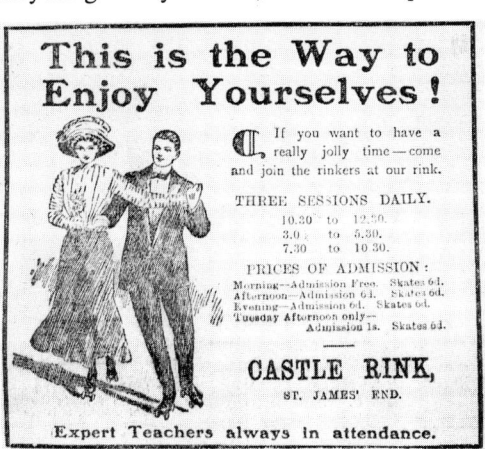

An advertisement for the Castle Rink.

While this was being constructed a race was going on at the other end of town to build a rival rink and to open it sooner. This was the Castle Rink on the corner of St. James's Park Road and West Bridge. This was a project undertaken by the Northampton firm of Henry Green for the General Rinks Company Ltd. at a contract price of £1,987. The building was completed in one month and consisted of a galvanised iron cladding on steel framework, the inside lined with matchboarding. Just 190 feet in length and 80 feet wide, the slightly

Staff of the American Roller Rink at Abington. The lady instructor, seated third from left, was unusual...and very popular!

smaller rink surface was surrounded by a ten-foot promenade with tea-rooms, cloakrooms, dais for the band, and an area for non-skaters, all raised above floor level.

The third rink rapidly being run up, in the meantime, was at the back of the George Hotel in George Row. This ambitious brick and steel structure held two rinks, one small one for learners 50 feet by 45 feet, and the principal one 110 feet by 55 feet. Handsomely appointed with tea-rooms panelled in oak and stained glass windows, it even had a garage underneath it capable of housing 60 cars. At the opening a councillor pointed out that the merry bells rang out from the neighbouring All Saints church, and that he hoped that they would be the precursors of the merry belles who would use the rink (sic).

At Franklin's Gardens a rink of sorts was already operating and attracting huge attendances.

The race to open first was won by the Castle Rink, which was launched by the mayor Councillor John Brown on Friday night, 7th May, 1909, with the American Rink opening with less ceremony the following afternoon.

Spectators described the scene at the Castle Rink with "poor Brown going along on his back hair, in the corner Jones skinning his knees and nose, while in the centre a kaleidoscope of arms and legs was sorting itself out". Others, however, were "gliding along backwards, conversing with the lady instructor, or ambling along on the forewheels only". It was amusing, too, we are told, to observe several types of English beauty who swept on the rink with supercilious glances, which soon gave way to frantic anxiety struggling through flushed faces when the skates began to have a little game to themselves. Several young ladies were not above falling, some said purposely, into the embraces of the male skating instructor.

One observer wrote that, "It is not a hard task to get down on the floor. The difficulty arises when one wants to get up. To try and rise in an orthodox way is futile. I saw one benighted individual going backwards on all fours at six miles an hour in a vain effort to gain the perpendicular. It is better to sit still, smile, and wait for the attendants to come to the rescue....And when falling, have a care what you clutch!"

Spectators were entertained, finally, by an exhibition of trick and fancy skating by Miss Lily Franks the champion child skater of America.

At Abington, the American Rink offered the use of the famous "Winslow" ball bearing roller skates and skating to the accompaniment of a military band. At the afternoon sessions admission was 6d for men, ladies free, with loan of skates 1/-.

Competition between these two rinks was fierce, and the following week both establishments decided to hold fancy dress skating carnivals on the same Thursday night. To sweet music, it was said, skaters of both sexes in costumes fanciful and fantastic, glided smoothly and gracefully. At the Castle, the band under Mr. Charles Tysoe played for dancing, a football match on skates was played between a Northampton team and one from Crystal Palace, won by the latter with two goals to nil, and a skating pushball match with a ball five feet in diameter provided much amusement. The amateur champion roller skater of England, Mr. Walter Stanton, gave a display. When it came to the fancy dress judging a surprise was waiting for the adjudicators. After making the awards, one entrant dressed as a Turkish harem girl and passed over by the judges, was revealed as a young man wearing cleverly applied make-up.

The carnival at the American Rink, meanwhile, was slightly more upmarket in that the skaters were not only in fancy dress, but also wore traditional domino masks. A Miss Allman of Gold Street won a prize with a patchwork Pierette outfit, while Mr. Hornby of Phippsville won a prize as a golliwog. Mr. E.W. Sykes, disguised as a Dutchman, skated around with skates attached to a pair of wooden clogs.

As well as these diversions the rinks catered for the sporting skater by arranging speed skating races, roller hockey matches, and even cricket on skates!

The mainly wooden rink at Abington was burned down in a disastrous fire in 1914 and the site is now occupied by a nice detached house. The Castle Rink became the Roxy Cinema and the Dover Hall. The George Rink site later housed a car showroom, a paint warehouse, and now serves, variously, as a hairdressers and a night club.

Just before World War II a fine roller skating rink was opened in Broad Street, in

The American Rink burnt down in 1914, this is all that remained the morning following the fire.

recent years the premises becoming an outpost of the Rest Assured bedding firm. With a fine sprung maple floor, it was place popular with adults and children alike. When war broke out, however, the rink was requisitioned by the army and used as a mess hall for the many soldiers billeted in the town. Their hobnailed boots chopped up the wooden floor irreparably and it was never reopened as a rink.

The George Rink was situated at the rear of the George Hotel. The entrance can be seen to the left, below the white sign advertising its facilities.

Then, after the war, a chapel at the top end of Abington Street, opposite the Mounts, was converted to a roller rink. One serious snag with this building was that the supporting columns of the gallery came down into the rink area, an unwary skater travelling backwards, perhaps, would collide with a sickening thud with these stanchions.

In recent years skating has made a comeback, reappearing as street-dance and disco.

Where Priests Hid For Their Lives

Roman Catholics were having a rough time, in England, as the 17th Century dawned. Elizabeth I was on the throne, and she had passed an Act which forbade any member of the Church of Rome from celebrating rites. Penalties were severe, though not as bad as they were later to become, forfeiture of property for the first offence, one year's prison for a second offence and imprisonment for life for a third.

Recusants, those who refused to take the Oath of Supremacy, were considered guilty of high treason. Any Papist who converted a Protestant to Rome would suffer death, as would the convert.

After the Gunpowder Plot in 1605, James I, two years into his reign, enforced the law against the Catholics with great vigour and severity.

Harrowden Hall from the air. The house is now the clubhouse of the Wellingborough Golf Club.

Many of the great families of Northamptonshire were Catholic and their large country estates were remote enough not only to provide ideal meeting places for religious celebrations, but to hide away priests on the run from pursuivants, state officials charged with capturing them. The Vauxs, Catesbys, Treshams, Fermors and Digbys were all involved in Catholic intrigue, members of many of them being arraigned before the Court of the Star Chamber for their complicity.

Despite the penalties, and the fact that they were proscribed, there were still many Catholic priests either attached to important families as chaplains, or travelling the countryside administering to believers and they needed hiding places as refuges from pursuers. Many of the county's mansions were modified to include secret rooms, chambers and escape routes, now generally known as "priest-holes".

Many of these, and certainly the most ingenious, were constructed by Nicholas Owens, a Jesuit lay brother and a servant of Father Henry Garnet, the Provincial of the English Jesuits. A Cockney carpenter, small in stature and with a deformed leg that made him limp, he was known throughout the Papist underground as Little John, working alone and often at night, removing masonry and altering woodwork to preserve secrecy. He was eventually captured at Hindlip Hall, in Worcestershire after Bates, a servant of the Catesby family of Ashby St. Ledgers, had betrayed him. He was taken to the Tower of London and tortured on the rack, dying during the interrogation.

The hall at Great Harrowden, now the home of Wellingborough Golf Club, was the ancient seat of the Vaux family, a notorious sanctuary for persecuted priests, and a centre for Catholic meetings. In 1598 priest John Gerard, 2nd son of Sir Thomas Gerard, a Lancashire knight, was sent as chaplain to Elizabeth Vaux, a widow with six children. Harrowden Hall was much dilapidated at this time, as was another of her houses at Irthlingborough, so she took the lease of Kirby Hall, a residence owned by Sir Christopher Hatton, the Lord Chancellor.

Kirby Hall soon attracted the attention of officialdom and was searched, so Father Gerard and Little John were sent to Harrowden to examine the fabric and assess the possibility of making it habitable and of incorporating hiding places. By the time Elizabeth Vaux moved in, the mansion was ideal for the gathering of large congregations and the celebration of mass. It housed a secret printing press operated by Henry Owen, brother of Nicholas, for the production of forbidden tracts and books. She even founded a Jesuit College here under the noses of the pursuivants.

Gerard, however, had attracted the attention of the Earl of Salisbury, the Lord Chief Justice of England, who gave orders that he should be captured at all costs and that Harrowden, which had already survived numerous searches, should be scoured until he was found. William Tate was dispatched with Sir Richard Chetwode, Sir William Samuel and Sir Robert Hartwell and a body of over 100 well armed men to attend to it. They met, initially at Delapre, at the house of Tate, before setting off for Harrowden as unobtrusively as possible. They arrived stealthily between 12 and 1 o'clock on Tuesday 12th of November, 1605 and set guards all around the house with patrols on all roads within a three mile radius. Then the search began.

The servants were first removed and a guard placed on Lady Vaux. As each room was searched it was locked and the key handed personally to Tate. Letters were ransacked, cupboards and trunks emptied and coffers of linen overturned. Candles were inserted in any crack or crevice found.

Continuously for five days the probe went on, but still they found nothing. Father Gerard, meanwhile, was cramped in a "hole within a hole" in the west wing of the house, stooped and unable to stand. Tate, writing to Salisbury to report his lack of success, was instructed to remain there and starve the priest out.

Lady Vaux, despite her custody, still managed to get food and water to Gerard, indeed, in the latter days of the search she even managed to get him out to stretch his legs before the fire at night. It was a stand-off! For ten days Tate's men roamed the house and still they found nothing. By now, too, the interrogation of the servants was becoming more brutal so, hoping to distract the searchers, Lady Vaux arranged for a manservant, Richard Richardson, to reveal one of the hiding places. He led Tate to a secret room behind some panelling, but nothing incriminating was found beyond a few Popish books and pamphlets. Little did he know that Gerard lay a wall's thickness beyond the chamber. The discovery was not enough to remove the surveillance, though.

Meanwhile, outside, a secular priest, Thomas Laithwood, had arrived trying to reach Gerard, but had been captured. Taken to a nearby inn for questioning, he escaped. Leaving his sword and cloak to allay suspicion, he swam a stream and galloped off into the night, only to get lost, ride back into a search party, and be recaptured.

By Sunday, Tate was losing patience and it was decided to arrest Elizabeth Vaux and her son and take her to London. Here she was examined by Lord Salisbury and a group of commissioners including the Earl of Northampton and eventually released.

The Dower House, Fawsley, where a printing press was housed in a secret room for the printing of "seditious" tracts and books.

The secret room and priest hole still survive in the fabric of the house, though they are in a part of the building used as living accommodation and have been boarded up.

Another of the Vaux family houses in Hackney had a similar double priest hole high in a wall under the overhang of a gable.

With Lady Vaux's lease of Kirby Hall it is almost certain that she had something to do with the huge secret chamber at Deene Park, just 1½ miles away. This chamber is large enough to contain a score of people. By releasing the panelling inside access is obtained to an underground passage that leads in the direction of Kirby Hall.

Most of these Northamptonshire catholics had some degree of involvement with the Gunpowder Plot, either actively or by association. The conspirators assembled in the half-timbered room above the gateway of Ashby St. Ledgers House, owned by the Catesbys. Robert, a son, was said to be the ringleader. As you would expect, the room had a secret door leading to an escape route.

The Dower House at Fawsley is now a ruin in imminent danger of collapsing into rubble, but it once had a secret room above the main hall where a printing press was housed. Political and religious tracts were produced here for distribution over a wide area, the house lying in a secluded valley where the noise of a press would not attract attention.

Northwest of Rothwell is Rushton Hall, now occupied by the Royal National Institute for the Blind. This was owned by one of the most prominent Catholic families in the whole of Britain, the Treshams. Sir Thomas Tresham built, in the grounds, the extraordinary and beautiful Triangular Lodge to signify the Holy Trinity. Three sided, each 33 feet long carrying three gables, every feature being in threes or multiples of three, the whole decorated with symbols of his religion. Legend has it that a tunnel was discovered running from the Lodge towards the Hall, and that, secretly, a local worthy paid a fiddler to walk the passage playing as he went, hoping to discover its route. As the sound faded there was a rumble and

Rushton Hall, just north of Kettering, where lived the Treshams, one of the country's foremost Catholic families.

the tunnel caved in. Unable to excavate such a huge collapse the doorway was filled in and never reopened, the fiddler being entombed there to this day.

According to old books, in the Great Hall was a priest-hole behind the large fireplace

The entrance to the tunnel at Rushton.

The tunnel at Rushton Hall.

in which Father Oldcorn, a recusant priest, was hidden. The present fireplace, though large and magnificent, is of a later date. Even though the hearth bricks bear a 16th century date and are obviously original, there is very little room between them and the buttressed external chimneypiece to accommodate any secret cavity, quite apart from the probability of cooking the priest when a fire was in use! There are other large and beautiful Elizabethan fireplaces in nearby rooms, perhaps the priesthole is behind one of them?

What certainly exists is an exciting tunnel that can be entered from the cellars. This was found by a Desborough historian a few years ago after a clever bit of detective work and the reading of infra red aerial photographs. How the original entrance was disguised is not clear, but we now enter it via a hole torn through the modern brick. The passageway is about four feet high and three feet wide with a vaulted roof and slopes gently upwards for some thirty feet. At the end it becomes a largish cavity in the loose earth, but, by looking up, one can see a stoneclad lining indicating that it was once possible to climb vertically. On the first floor i.e. two rooms above the tunnel, there is the oratory, a small chamber

Some of the items found in the tunnel and hole at Rushton Hall.

Old books say that a secret chamber was used to hide Father Oldcorn and was behind the fireplace of the Great Hall at Rushton. The external dimensions of the stack, however, suggest that it was altered when a later fireplace was fitted.

for private devotion that carries on its end wall a remarkable religious panel depicting the crucifixion moulded in full relief from composition and bearing the date 1577. Certain doorways and niches for holy water have been covered in, now, but it seems certain that priests using the tunnel could once climb up through the thickness of the wall and emerge in the tiny chapel.

When cleared, the tunnel yielded many oyster shells, animal bones and bits of ancient bottles, possibly remnants of sustenance passed to the outlawed priests. Amongst the debris, too, was a tiny sanctus bell dated 1580.

In 1832, during some alterations, another secret place was found over a doorway, behind a lintel, with access from the floor above. It was full of old manuscripts, prohibited books and incriminating correspondence of the Treshams.

Even though small objects of Catholic devotion were forbidden there grew up in the county a thriving cottage industry for the making of rosaries and suchlike. Houses, while not containing priest-holes, often had secret compartments to house religious artifacts. Castle Ashby had one such which swivelled on pivots to reveal the contents.

Though not actually in Northamptonshire, and thus not strictly within County Tales, the house at Compton Wynyates is owned by the Comptons, Earls of Northampton. It had the most extraordinary series of secret hideaways. Ostensibly they were a Protestant family, indeed, there was a fine Protestant chapel on the ground floor. In the roof above it, though, was concealed a Popish chapel with several secret escape routes. Between the huge timber beams and the wainscot were several secret closets. In the roof around the courtyard were a number of cramped rooms.

One tiny apartment was known as The Devil's Chamber; another, when discovered lately, contained a skeleton. Still more held a

The lintel at Rushton Hall in 1832 behind which was discovered a secret hiding place full of incriminating documents and proscribed literature.

quantity of Compton papers, while one has the reputation of being haunted, the window when closed at night, is always found to be open the next morning.

An unusual feature is a cunning trap for unwary searchers. One room was originally only accessible by ladder, but this hindered quick entrance, so the construction was altered to include a secret passageway. This had a removable floor so that, in the dark, any unsuspecting pursuer would plummet through the hole to his death.

Near Newport Pagnell, tucked away in a fold of the countryside, and only ¾ mile from Tyringham, owned by another of the Catesby family, is Gayhurst, then known as Gothurst. It is a fine late Tudor building, once the seat of Sir Everard Digby, one of the greatest landowners in the East Midlands with a reputation as a wild sportsman in his youth, having been caught poaching in Staffordshire, been expelled from his Cambridge college for blowing a hunting horn and hallooing loudly in the court, and having written the first ever book, fully illustrated, on the art of swimming. He received his knighthood from the King in 1603, but became a zealous Catholic convert. He knew of the Gunpowder Plot, indeed, Guy Fawkes had visited the house during October, and it is said that, on November 5th Digby lay in the field at his estate with his ear pressed to the ground listening for the tremor of the great explosion.

One of the plotters fleeing north came to the house where, in one apartment, there was a secret room. This chamber was an unusual one in that it admitted light and air via

Gayhurst, near Newport Pagnell, once the home of Sir Everard Digby, one of the supporters of the Gunpowder Plot.

part of a tall mullioned window, a false ceiling separating it from the normal room below. A secret passage in the thickness of the wall communicated with it and led to the cellars. Entrance was also possible by means of movable flooring and a revolving hearthstone in the room above that swung away on a pivot and was thick and heavy enough to sound solid and thus allay suspicion. A hidden bolt in the floor of this compartment, in turn, released a panel and disclosed a further hiding place.

This chamber was over the porch on the east front of the house. A square, solid, projection is in the middle of this wing and it was the upper half of the room on the first floor that was converted into the secret room.

The story goes that the house was surrounded and searched with no success so, at night, the commander of the searchers gave orders that his men were to light a candle in every window. Word was, somehow, passed to the fugitive, and he also lit a candle. What he did not know, though, was that a secret order had been given to the searchers, and on a pre-arranged signal all the candles were extinguished and the hiding placed revealed.

Some legends state that this man was Digby himself, but history records that he was arrested at Holbeach House, where Catesby and Percy were mown down with a hail of musket shot. Sir Everard went to the Tower for his part in the plot and after being tortured, was hung, drawn and quartered.

This remarkable priest's hole was destroyed just before the First World War when Lord Carrington carried out modernisation at Gayhurst and had the false ceiling torn down and the passageway blocked up. At the far end of the house was another secret chamber some eight feet square sandwiched between the first and second floors. This, together with a hidden chapel in the roofspace, known as the oratory, which had a window masked from outside by a blank wall, has been lost due to reconstruction work in the house.

All that now survives of the many secret passages and rooms that once riddled this house, is part of a tunnel in one of the cellars.

Music Hall Lived On In Clubs

All the history books say that Music Hall died with the coming of Variety, when the licensed bar took over from the licensed hall. Most will put the date around the time of the First World War. I believe, though, that the Music Hall lived on for at least another thirty years, in the Working Men's Clubs.

Most of the dozen or so Working Men's Clubs in Northampton had their concert halls. The one at St. James's End W.M.C. was typical. Reached by a substantial stone staircase round three sides of the square foyer and through a pair of swing doors, it was a lofty hall some 75 feet long. At the opposite end of the hall was the stage, quite small and flanked by two dressing rooms barely 7' x 7' that were a squeeze for any act to prepare in, so were crammed to capacity when a dance troupe, for instance, was making up.

The backcloth represented a balustraded balcony and, beyond, an idyllic view of a lake in the middle of which was a wooded island. Frozen immobile in an attitude of nonchalance was a gondolier on the stern of a vaguely Venetian boat. It was before this incongruous scene that comics, acrobats, magicians, and jugglers, performed.

In the body of the hall on a softwood floor that was so worn down by working men's boots that the knots stood proud, cast-iron tables, bearing W.G. Grace's portrait, and chairs were arranged to seat some 170 or so people. A dais to one side of the stage was the jealously guarded domain of the chairman, a stout figure of imposing presence, whose authority was emphasised by means of sharp blows on a large bell, accompanied by cries of "Best of order....PLEASE!" Sycophants would, periodically, bring him frothing mugs of his favourite ale.

Waiters scurried about collecting and serving orders for beer, though they paused in deference to the more serious acts like singers or sentimental monologuists.

Children, I might add, were expected to be quiet and attentive, but, if well behaved, were allowed to occupy the only two rows of seats just below the stage.

Mostly the acts were local and we knew their routines off by heart. Florence Someo (a name famous locally for the delicious ice cream sold by other members of her artistically talented family) had a lovely operatic soprano voice. She always included her favourite song "Ceri, Ceribim".

Musical talent seemed to run in families. There were the Dawsons, mother Eva played the piano while husband Tom would black-up to sing, dance and play the clackers to "coon" songs. Their sons, Billy and George, played the drums and clarinet. George later teamed up with Clarrie White to form a comedy duo.

Billed as Northampton's Nightingale, another fine singer was Phyllis Gammage.

Then there was Ted Toone who sang light popular music.

Popular, too, were the Civil family, each a master of a musical instrument. Alan, one of the sons went on to become a world famous instrumentalist.

Another family whose name hit the headlines were the Loudens. Tommy Louden played the drums, his wife the piano, but it was their beautiful tap-dancing daughter June who made news when she twice won the title "Northampton's Pocket Venus" at the New Theatre.

When I think of dancers of that time I think of Fred and Frances with their stylish Astaire-type numbers. They later turned 'pro'.

There was, inevitably, the monologuist who staggered around the stage with a bloody bandage round his head to recite "There's a One-Eyed Yellow Idol to the North of Katmandu".

My favourites, however, were Askew and Frisby, a comedy couple along the lines of Flanagan and Allen. Edgar Frisby was the dignified straight man, suave and clad in impeccable dinner jacket, and was harassed by the quick-fire repartee of partner Harry Askew, dressed in short-legged, loudly-checked suit and wearing his "trademark", a battered trilby hat folded to a point at the front *à la* Arthur Askey. Askew's make-up was pale almost to the white of a clown, with a red blob in the corner of each eye. We kids loved his irreverent, and slightly rude, comedy. The duo were good enough, anyway, to have appeared on the professional stage at the New Theatre, in Abington Street, on several occasions, notably as the robbers in Babes in the Wood. They frequently gave their services at charity shows all over the Midlands during the war, one memorable performance being at the Exchange Cinema when they played second billing to Mantovani and his Orchestra.

Comic double-act Askew and Frisby, stalwarts of the clubs and popular entertainers on the professional circuit.

Comics abounded on the clubs, and the styles were widely varied. Jack Ablett (and it's hard to imagine him as the man who later earned local renown as a dignified, scarlet-tailed, master of ceremonies), was an exponent of eccentric dancing in the style of Nat Jackley, the rubber-legged comedian. A comedian with a risque, one might justifiably say "blue", routine was Frank Victor, who worked in drag.

Magicians, in particular, had a difficult time in the clubs, the stages generally being very small and the lighting primitive. One such act, I remember, whose speciality was the production of pastel coloured doves, saw his birds fly off to perch high on the tie-rods of the open, barn-type, roof where they cooed noisily throughout the rest of the programme, his attempts to recapture them at the end of the evening being almost as amusing as his act.

Local artistes Reg Gayton and wife Mabs were but one outstanding magic act that performed on Northampton club stages between engagements in top-class variety.

Some of the entertainers who polished their skills on the boards of Working Men's Clubs went on to fame and fortune. The Munks Twins, Nancy and Molly, and Des O'Connor, among them.

One act which made it's debut on the Working Mens Club stage was The Coram Twins and Joy. The twins, Teddy and Babs, were about fifteen, and had just started work at the Chronicle & Echo. They achieved fame and fortune as The Beverley Sisters.

Every now and then, punctuating the regular concerts, was a "Free and Easy", at which anyone who had a mind to could take the stage and perform. Club members who had, perhaps, only one party-piece would trot it out. Of course, everyone knew who did what and would call loudly for their favourites, while the chairman would make the big introduction.

Thus we heard some strange musicians, whistlers trilling to the accompaniment of "In a Monastery Garden", instrumentalists bowing away on a wood saw or a phonofiddle, or clacking away with bones or spoons. It was here that we kids learned the many verses of "My Brother Sylvest" and "Working Outside the Lunatic Asylum", verses that remain in my mind to this day.

Not least of the skilled performers who inhabited the clubs was the piano-accompanist, who could make or break an act. Men such as Ted Malin and Arthur Pollard. Arthur Pollard was known as the Mad Musician and was a great composer of marches.

The old-style Working Men's Club concert faded away with the coming of television and with the increasing wealth of many of the clubs. Emulating the cabaret-style shows on T.V., the chairman gave way to the on-stage compere, waiter service ceased, and even the proscenium and painted backdrop disappeared.

From Beyond The Grave.....

Guidance from beyond the grave was said to be behind the finding of a hoard of money in a Northamptonshire village over 100 years ago. Sir Charles Isham, of Lamport Hall, a noted spiritualist, investigated the case and examined the "facts" recorded in a number of statements.

Barby, to the west of the county, was the village where lived an old lady, Mrs. Webb. She was the widow of a man of property who had left her pretty well off upon his death, although she showed little evidence of wealth, having the reputation in the village of being mean. Even so, neighbours rallied round when she became ill, two women, in particular, attending to her needs and nursing her, while a local farmer, Mr. Hart, provided food, etc. Despite their care, however, Mrs. Webb died on March 3rd, 1851.

Her house, which she had left in her will to Mr. Hart, was empty, but a month after Mrs Webb's passing strange noises were heard at dead of night from within the building. Mrs Holding, who lived next door, described heavy thumps, the dragging noise of furniture being moved, and the door of the wall-cupboard being slammed.

Mr. Hart was anxious to let the house, and Mr. and Mrs. Accleton with their ten year-old daughter, being desperate for accommodation, took the place, despite the talk of hauntings. The whole family slept in the room in which Mrs. Webb had died. At night, usually about the same time, 2 am, they were often awakened by strange and eerie noises, heavy footsteps, the violent crash of weighty furniture, and, worst of all, ghastly moans.

Then, one night, the child shattered the night with her screams, "Mother, there's a tall woman standing by my bed shaking her head at me".

Again that night the apparition appeared to the child, and several times on subsequent nights. Only the child saw the ghost of Mrs. Webb. Until, that is, one night when Mrs Accleton, her husband being away on business, had her mother Mrs. Radbourne staying with her. The women were both awakened by a bright luminous glow in the room and in the light appeared clearly the figure of Mrs. Webb advancing towards them with hands stretched out imploringly. The spectre seemed to be agitated and wore an expression of desperation. Unable to communicate, it faded away.

It next appeared before a small group of the neighbours, including Mrs. Accleton, her mother, Mrs Holding and Mrs. Griffiths. Again the luminous wraith materialised, but now with spheres of light travelling from its ghostly figure to the trapdoor in the roof of the cottage. The vision was accompanied by eerie moanings and agonised groans.

Mrs. Webb's legendary miserliness and the notably small wealth found upon her death led, naturally perhaps, to a discussion about hidden money and the conclusion was reached that the ghost was trying to tell them something about it's hiding place.

The owner of the cottage and it's occupant, Mr. Hart and Mrs. Accleton, together searched the attic indicated by the spectral emanations and found, to their great surprise, a bundle of documents, deeds, and a large bag of gold coins and banknotes.

It was assumed, now, that the ghostly manifestations would cease, but no, the disturbances continued with the phantom figure becoming increasingly agitated, plainly frustrated with it's inability to communicate. Mr. Hart, however, remembered how religiously Mrs. Webb had paid every bill and debt throughout her life, being obliged to no-one.

Using the treasure to pay off a number of Mrs. Webb's small outstanding debts revealed in the documents, the house at Barby at long last settled into silence. Mrs. Webb's ghost returned to eternal rest and was never seen again.

Abington's Pierrots

How many people are there who remember the little band of pom-pommed pierrots that performed at Abington? Not at the park's bandstand; that was reserved for much grander musicians; but on a piece of waste ground roughly where Abington Motors Garage is today, a venue referred to in the advertisements of the day as Abington Park Gates.

The pierrot show enjoyed immense popularity up until the First World War and survived in modified form right through into the Thirties. These shows had their roots in the nigger minstrel shows that had entertained seaside visitors from the 1860s. The format

The pierrots perform at Abington Park Gates.

was more or less standard. The entire company would sit in a semicircle while the performers went through their individual acts at the front of the stage. The comic, usually with some quaint name like Mr. Bones, exchanged repartee with the compere, or interlocutor, both of whom acted as linkmen for the show.

Then, in the 1890s, the minstrels were ousted by a more upmarket group, the concert party. A band of concert singers and classical instrumentalists, wearing immaculate evening dress and masked to hide their true identities, started it all.

The next step came when a group adopted the all-enveloping costume of the French pierrot character, with giant pom-poms and white make-up. They performed before the Prince of Wales on the Isle of White and became the Royal Pierrots. The style was widely copied.

The pierrot's performances were not confined to the beach, however, for paid holidays for workers were far from common, and there was a ready-made audience among the stay-at-homes. Thus, in 1905, Northampton saw the arrival of the Grapho and Jackson troupe. Early on they tried a number of titles, the Chez Les Pierrots, The Mascots, among others, but pretty soon they settled for the Jovial Jollies, a name that served for several

Grapho's Chez Les Mascots perform at Abington Park Gates in 1906

decades.

Bertie Grapho (he usually billed himself more grandly as Mr. Herbert Grapho) was a skilled lightning artist, executing quick caricatures of prominent people, as well as an accomplished comedian. Billy Jackson, his partner in the enterprise, was a pianist. Both had started their stage careers with Mulvana's Minstrels, a blackfaced troupe, back in the Nineties.

Their Northampton season, in those early days, extended from May to September and was in an open-air enclosure on a field alongside Christchurch.

As well as the regular members of the troupe, such favourites as La Tagarte "the famous Italian baritone", Theodore Jones, Sam Hilton and Mr Pino Conti the "humorist", special attractions were booked. Thus, in August 1907, we find Joe Hennessy the club juggler, and the Royal Victoria Boys who were international dancers, on the programme "warming the house" for top of the bill Zasma the Society Gymnast.

As live entertainment was then battling with the bioscope craze, each Grapho and

Bert Grapho.

Jackson performance also included a series of "animated pictures". In wet weather the show was transferred to the stage of the Temperance Hall, in the lower part of Newland.

Each regular artiste in the troupe would have a benefit show during the season. At the end of the summer a grand final show and a "pierrot dance" would take place at the Temperance Hall and, if the weather looked like holding, Bertie Grapho would bring down his other troupe from Walsall, called the Merry Mascots, for a special one week guest visit.

Grapho exercised his showmanship with every trick in the book to attract audiences. He frequently included established local favourites in the cast, Tony Black "Northampton's Favoured Scotch Comedian" for example, and, during the 1911 season, engaged sixteen local children in two "picturesque concerted numbers" that packed them in.

It was in 1911 that Grapho took over part of the nearby roller skating rink as a theatre and winter garden. The American Rink stood at the corner of Ardington Road and Wellingborough Road, just across the road from the Abington Park Hotel. A large wooden structure that had opened with great ceremony two years earlier, it was leased to Grapho, who added six tiers of seats bringing the seating up to 1,500. A cafe was included and roller skating was still possible between shows. Opened as Grapho's Winter Gardens on Monday 16th October 1911 by the mayor, the first show starred Captain Permane's Teddy Bears, "the acme of animal intelligence", together with Kate and Dorothy Hughes "the clever juveniles in their drawing room speciality".

Following on at the Winter Gardens there came a spectacular show fresh from Crystal Palace, "Wild Australia". Part of this show included an "unrideable" bucking mule, a prize of £5 awaiting any successful rider. One local hero, a Mr O.G. Chamberlain of 22, Cromwell Street, who had had some experience of mules during army service in India, having driven them harnessed to Maxim guns, essayed the task and stayed on for 38 seconds, the previous best being a mere 4½ seconds. He collected his fiver, however, amid accusations of a trick.

Then, in 1914, a disastrous fire consumed the Winter Gardens, destroying it totally. It being wartime, the place was never reconstructed.

Bertie Grapho decided to put concert parties on tour, his shows becoming particularly popular at the Scottish seaside resorts. While performing near Glasgow he saw a child entertainer, Jack McAlpine, and took him into the Jovial Jollies. Eventually the boy was adopted by the Graphos and became part of the family, using the name Jack Grapho.

Bertie Grapho died in the late 1920s, but Jack Grapho, or Wee Jackie as he was known, continued running the Jovial Jollies together with Bertie's widow, presenting regular summer shows at Saltburn, as they had since 1899. The troupe carried on until 1939

Grapho's Jovial Jollies, the alternative to the pierrot show.

Northampton's Horse Racing Course

A bugle call rang out and the line of horsemen charged forward to the roar of a thousand voices. It sounds like the Charge of the Light Brigade, but the scene is Northampton Racecourse.

It could have been any year from 1652 to 1904, for that was how long this grassy common was used for horse racing.

The history of Northampton Races starts at Harlestone Heath, now the Firs, in 1632, when a series of horse races was instituted with the town's Corporation each year donating a trophy, the Harlestone Plate, with a value of £16. 13s. 4d. Racing continued there until 1734 when, due to a dispute with the landowners, it ceased.

Meanwhile, back in town, unofficial horse racing was taking place on a 118 acre site called Freeman's Common, now the Racecourse. Meetings became official in 1658, but lapsed from lack of interest, the Harlestone event being far more firmly established.

In 1727 racing was revived as the Althorp Park Stakes and the Spencer Plate on the,

The finishing straight with the grandstand, now the Pavilion Restaurant, beyond.

by now, properly laid out track on "the New Course". The meetings were usually held in September and lasted three days. Later a Spring meeting was added.

The threat of the Enclosure Acts caused a rift between the landowners and the corporation in 1758, with the owners forbidding racing. Racing did take place, though the row rumbled on for 20 more years until, in 1778, the Northampton Enclosure Act was passed, which awarded rights of herbage on the racecourse to the freemen of the town, but with express provision allowed for horse racing to continue.

The race meetings, at this time, were highlights of the local season with many social events held in connection with the races. Gentlemens Ordinaries, convivial dinners, were held at the Red Lion in Horsemarket. The Ladies Ordinary was held at The Peacock on the Market Square, while the climax came with the glittering Race Ball at the George Hotel on George Row.

The paddock with East Park Parade beyond.

By the beginning of the 19th century the races were firmly established, even though the Racecourse was still let out by the trustees for sheep grazing between November and February each year, during which time local citizens were barred from the area. Even the furze bushes which dotted the commons were sold by auction each year.

As the century went on the fame of Northampton Races attracted famous names and followers of the sport of kings. Squire Osbaldeston, the Pytchley MFH and notorious gambler, Jem Mason, Lord Chesterfield and, later, actress Lillie Langtry, the Prince of Wales (later King Edward VII), the Rothschilds, millionaire Austrian barons, and, of course, the Spencer family. Rubbing shoulders, too, were the card sharps, thimbleriggers, tipsters, and pickpockets, that were drawn to rich pickings. Violence sometimes erupted, on one occasion crowds chased a gipsy and set fire to his caravan with him still in it. To accommodate arrested criminals until they could be marched into town, a small jail was built

Horses go to the start passing the race-board and finishing post in so doing.

adjoining the grandstand.

Up to 1882 freemen still had the right to graze cattle and sheep on the Racecourse, despite the inconvenience, so the Northampton Corporation Act was passed, paying trustees £80 per annum, and thus acquiring the ground for the town. It was this Act, too, that gained several other small commons and odd parcels of land as gardens and recreation grounds, and was the basis of Northampton's fine array of parks.

Also in 1882, as a sop, perhaps, to the trustees, the Corporation Purse, valued at £50, was instituted and competed for on the last day of each Michaelmas race meeting.

Local riders took part in many of the races there. Great excitement was generated at the Spring Meeting held at the end of March, 1898, when Bert Randall, an amateur jockey soon to turn professional, and the second son of Sir Henry Randall, mayor of Northampton and prominent shoe manufacturer of the town, rode in his very first horse race. On the second day he rode his father's horse Beverini to victory. The horse had already won a race the previous day, so was heavily backed by local punters.

The course was a tight one and was by now gaining a reputation as being dangerous. To get a 5 furlong straight the start was made near Leicester Street at the west end of the Racecourse, where fencing had to be temporarily removed from the end of Bailiff Street. For the Stakes, the start was near the rear of the Militia Fields (now the Drill Hall), and covered just over a lap.

The 1901 meeting saw two local jockeys, Sam Loakes and Frank Hardy, both involved in serious accidents. Loakes was riding Nateby in the autumn races when a small child wandered on to the course. The boy's father, one Samuel Smith of St. Michael's Mount, rushed forward to recover the child, but was struck by Nateby. The crash also brought down Sun Bonnet ridden by Bert Randall and Queen Theo ridden by a jockey called Dainty. Loakes suffered a broken thigh and fractured ribs. Samuel Smith received compound fractures of his skull, a broken leg, and other injuries from which he never recovered, dying some time later.

The final blow to the races came in 1904, by which time the Jockey Club was worried about the danger of Northampton's unfenced, uneven, course criss-crossed, as it was, by well worn footpaths.

The Spring Meeting on 30th and 31st March saw a programme of six races each day. The big race of the first day was the Earl Spencer Plate, a handicap over 5 furlongs for 250 guineas, won by a horse called Milleray at 3 to 1. Leonard de Rothschild's Catgut was second and L'Brassey's Arabi third. The Northampton Stakes, the main race of the day, was a longer race over one mile and five furlongs for 400 sovereigns. Jupiter Pluvius was first past the winning post but was disqualified for passing the wrong side of a marker, called a dolly, that was the only thing that distinguished the course in the outfield, and the race was awarded to Grand Deacon.

During the meeting, in an event called the Kelmarsh Plate, Frank Hardy, another local pro jockey, rode into a bend near Bailiff Street on Mr. S. Pickering's horse Traitress. The animal slipped on loose tan that was used to cover a footpath and hit one of the dolly markers, somersaulting into a knot of spectators and crushing Mr. Passmore and his son. The race was won by a filly called Lucrecia Borgia ridden by Kempton Cannon.

The last race of that spring meeting turned out to be the last race ever on the Racecourse. It was the Delapre Welter Handicap over six furlongs for 103 sovereigns and was won by Guilty, with Gridiron second and Mount Lyall third.

On Tuesday 27th September, 1904, the Jockey Club announced that Northampton Racecourse was no longer considered fit for racing, meetings were no more to be held there, and that, therefore, the autumn fixture was cancelled. Racing never took place there again.

Attempts were made to find an alternative venue and to run the meeting on land adjacent to the town, but they were not successful.

Carthorse Wins The Grand National

From pulling the local omnibus to the winners enclosure of the Grand National is a bigger jump than Beechers Brook, but a Northamptonshire owned horse once did just that.

It was in 1908 that it happened, much to the surprise of racing's so-called experts. Rubio was the horse's name and it was owned by Major E. Douglas-Pennant, who lived at Sholebrook Lodge, Towcester. The gallant major was an officer in the King's Royal Rifles and a popular rider to hounds with the Grafton Hunt. Rubio was an American bred horse, half brother to the great jumper Sceptre, so had, it was initially thought, great promise. After being brought to England as a yearling, Rubio was sold to Mr Septimus Clarke of Lillingstone Dayrell for fifteen guineas. He was rapidly sold on at a profit. The price, now, was 95 guineas, and the buyer Major Douglas-Pennant.

The horse, however, failed to live up to his pedigree, so Rubio was sent to the Leicester sales with a reserve price of sixty guineas on him. When the bidding failed to reach even this figure the animal was withdrawn, returned to the county, and sent to Mr. Bletsoe of Grendon, a well-established trainer who, as it happened, already had trained one Grand National winner, Grudon, in his stables.

At Grendon Rubio improved markedly, winning three successive races convincingly. Then, suddenly, his health broke down. His future looked black and he was loaned to Mr. O. Browning, the proprietor of the Pomfret Arms at Towcester, who put him to work between the shafts of the horse bus that ran hotel guests back and forth to Towcester railway station.

The work was hard but it worked wonders with Rubios suspect legs and after some months the horse was fit enough to be taken back into training. A season of hunting with the Grafton polished his jumping ability and an outing at the point-to-point, which he won, proved it.

When he was entered in the 1908 Grand National, ridden by the trainer's son H.B. Bletsoe, Rubio was a rank outsider, and even as the horses left the start the bookmakers were still offering 66 to 1 odds .... and there were not many takers!

Young Bletsoe, riding in his first Grand National, had an easy ride. He was seen several times to look round at following jockeys and laugh to see them vainly thrashing their mounts in an effort to catch Rubio. "I knew three fences from home that I only had to keep him on his legs to win," he later said, "He was not tiring at all, and jumped the last three fences as perfectly as a stag, and he pulled so fresh that I believe he could have gone another two miles".

The win was such a surprise that the Aintree crowd forgot to cheer, it was said, and very few local people had put any money on it. It was a great day for Major Douglas-Pennant, apart from the 3,000 sovereigns prize, for his wife, a native of Whittlebury, had entered her own horse Mattie McGregor in the race which had come home second to Rubio.

Northampton's Royal Park

History is all around us, and in the most unlikely places. Take Moulton Park, a bustling modern industrial estate of box-like factory units. An improbable site for a royal park? But that is what it was, and relics can still be seen.

Most of the royal Moulton Park was surrounded with a high stone wall enclosing 450 acres. It followed, roughly, the line of today's Boughton Lane from near Northampton Lane right round, in a sweeping curve, along the south side of Boughton Green Road to about where Nene College now stands. It then continued almost due south, across the area now called Parklands, towards the Kettering Road, near Manfield Hospital.

As early as 1250 Henry III issued a writ ordering the sheriff to enclose or fence the park and, when done, to inform him of the cost. Whether this was found to be a bit too expensive one does not know, but soon after we find that local villages were each allotted a length of wall and were made responsible for its upkeep and repair. The village name and the length of wall in its care was engraved on marker stones built into the structure.

Perhaps there was, at the outset, some resistance to the King's scheme for, in 1272, we find Edward I issuing orders that tenants must be made to maintain parts of the enclosure of Moulton Park "which they have neglected to do for sixteen years past".

The King himself, in those early years, assumed part of the responsibility for wall repairs himself, it seems, and certainly Edward II did, as confirmed in an order from Westminster dated 1307. The villagers, on their part, were more tardy, for in 1314 the king was forced to make an order to distrain others, without delay, for the repairs. Ten years later, in 1324, he ordered 20 shillings (£1) to be expended on repairs to the wall.

The wall was getting a bit ramshackle, it would appear, for a survey of the structure was ordered by the King in 1328 and keepers were told to get the work done "as the King understands that there are many defects to the wall".

Villages not wishing to provide men and materials to do the work themselves could meet their obligations by proxy, as it were, and pay for the work to be done. Payment came in slowly, so, in 1330 we find John Dandelyn the sheriff of the county and his predecessors fined for neglecting to oblige several villages to repair the wall. Robert Williams of Moulton, in a sworn statement in court said that many villages "to the number of six score do, and tyme out of minde have usyd to paye their rent yerely" to effect repairs. Among the 120 villages supposed to maintain the wall were Clipston, Crick, Deene, Drayton, Byfield, and Litchborough, all of whom paid 4d, Walgrave, Cransley, Orlingbury, Hannington, Moulton of course, and "dyverse other townshippes".

Some of the parishes that owed duty to the wall's repair probably found it a burden, and some idea of the costs can be obtained from some notes dated 1398 when two carters were hired at 1d a day, four masons at 3d a day, carts at 10d, and labourers at 1d a day, to help with maintenance.

The wall was important to keep in the royal deer and other animals. In 1228, during a period of the wall's neglect, peasants stock frequently wandered into the parkland to graze and a mandate was issued ordering the sheriff to turn out all beasts found in the park except those belonging to the King, and to keep pasture and herbage to fatten the King's oxen beasts for the royal larder in winter. This done and the wall repaired, the King restocked the park with game, and six years later we find John de Nevill, the chief forester, being ordered to take 20 buck and 60 does out of nearby Rockingham Forest to stock the King's Park at Northampton. The king would often make gifts of animals from the park to his favourites, as in 1274 when he sent four bucks from Moulton to the Archbishop of Canterbury.

Hares were also reared on the estate, thus we find 12 live hares being sent to Nicholas de Lukehoin in 1279 to stock his groves.

Despite severe penalties, poaching was not unheard of. Matthew Rugepull had his goods and chattels confiscated in 1278 for trespass, committed in chasing on the King's Warren and for taking hares without the King's licence. He was lucky to get away with his life. In 1292, though, the king generously gave a licence for life to one of his yeomen, one Almaricus, to hunt fox, badger, and hare, also cats, with his own dogs, except during fence-month, a period when it was unlawful to hunt, shoot, or fish, or take birds eggs. He was specifically forbidden, though, to take great game, or to hunt in the warrens.

The trees on the estate, too, were cultivated, and sometimes given as gifts. Sixteens oaks from Moulton Park, for instance, were donated for the repair of Northampton Castle in 1273, and, in 1275, one was given to Michael de Weston to repair Overstone Manor. Twelve leafless oak stumps (the order was carefully worded thus) were given to the Friar Preachers of Northampton in 1284 for fuel at their next provincial chapter to be held in the town.

That kings actually stayed at Moulton there is no doubt, for many documents exist with datelines issued from Moulton.

Two lodges existed in the park, The Great Lodge being roughly where Nene College stands today. This was virtually in Kingsthorpe, indeed in 1549 the keeper paid his offering to the parish church of Kingsthorpe and all persons dying out of the Great Lodge were buried at the parish church.

The villagers of Kingsthorpe certainly suffered at the hands of one of the keepers, one Robert Latham. He claimed the rights of freewarren, that is, the right to hunt conies (rabbits) and hares on common land outside the royal estate. Just to make sure that he had a worthwhile bag he knocked holes in the wall, allowing rabbits from the royal warrens to establish themselves on common lands in Kingsthorpe, Moulton, and Pitsford. So infested did these lands become that grazing was destroyed, beasts famished and up to a quarter of all corn eaten. The rabbits even established a warren in the old churchyard at Boughton Green, scatching up human bones until they lay thick on the ground. Latham was a violent man, known to cut the throats of villagers' dogs, even when they were upon a leash. "He did belte one Thomas Betts and brake hys head", says a contemporary report. When Kingsthorpe men ploughed land near the warrens during nesting time, Latham cut the plough harness.

An appeal was made by the people of Kingsthorpe to the Star Chamber in 1634, three local men travelling to London to protest. They stayed for three weeks at a cost of £9. 17s. 7d, money raised by selling plate, ironwork and wax from the parish church.

Moulton Park is no stranger to murder, either, for in 1322 a search was instituted for the persons who killed John Wake of Deping there. In 1327 Edward III issued a pardon for Roger Marshall of Moulton and his accomplices, the two sons of Hugh of Moulton, who were found guilty of the death of two men in the Park, on the condition that they joined the army fighting against the Scots. Similarly, another Moulton man, Robert Hacuvany, was pardoned for the death of John of Moulton, in recognition of his good service in the wars against France.

It seems that the estate went out of royal ownership during the reign of Charles II, and by 1791 was in the hands of the Thursby family, residents of Abington Manor. From the Thursbys it passed to Lord Lilford until, in 1908, we find parts of it in the possession of St. Andrew's Hospital. The two Lodges survived until about 1861, when one was entirely demolished and the other converted into farm buildings.

The ancient ivy-covered wall still marks part of the boundary of the old Royal Park and some of the structure of the lodges are incorporated in buildings in the area. Other than that, only names provide a link with the past. There once was a shelter in the thicket called Summerhouse Spinney, close by what is now called Summerhouse Road, and there are names like Deer Park Road and King's Park Road to recall the past.

The Great School War

When I went to St. James's Church of England School it was a fairly tranquil educational backwater. I often wondered, though, why the school area seemed to be bisected by a railed wall, passage through it being by means of a narrow gateway. Little did I then realise that this marked the division between the original old school and the later extensions, featured in the Great School War that reverberated around the St. James's End suburb in 1899.

The St. James's Church Schools, as they were then called, had been opened since 1866, when the land had been given for the purpose by the Reverend William Thornton of Kingsthorpe Hall. Church of England services were held in the school rooms until such time as the church itself was built. It was always a tough school, in an area noted for strong, free-thinking, craftsmen. The first school inspector in 1866 wrote that "the boys who attend this school are so unruly that the Master must exercise the utmost firmness and good temper to bring them to the proper habits of discipline."

That Master must have done a good job, for a year later he was reporting that "the cane has not been used all week."

By 1898 the school had grown to a remarkable size, with some 1,100 pupils cramming the small classrooms which seemed to be bursting at the seams. Religious instruction, naturally, was rigid Church of England, and it was this that bothered the many non-conformist families in the locality who were forced to send their children to this, the only school in the area. They felt that their offspring were being indoctrinated in the established church dogma.

There was a "Conscience Clause" which allowed parents to withdraw their children from any religious observance or instruction, but an increasing cry was raised for the establishment of a new Board School under properly elected representatives rather than the vicar, the Rev. W.P. Hurrell.

In May 1898 the adjacent Dallington and Duston School Board called for a new school to be provided under public control. With the overcrowding at the Church School, and an ever-increasing number of pupils requiring teaching, they felt that they had a good case.

To their surprise, they found that the church authorities had stolen a march on them, and that extensions to the existing Church School were already planned and well in hand. The "Jimmy's Enders", largely non-conformists, were furious. Petitions were organised, public meetings held, and protests rallied.

War was declared by a minister, the Reverend Jabez Bell, who was supported by one

Rebellious parents and children mill about on Cafe Square, St. James's End, after pupils had been turned away from the church school in January 1899.

of the most powerful figures in St. James's End at that time, the shoe factory owner Mr. T.D. Lewis. The St. James's Education League was formed to campaign for the establishment of a Board School free of church controls.

Allegations and counter-allegations flew back and forth concerning pressure and coercion of parents by Lewis and the non-conformists, and by the vicar and churchmen. The sectarians claimed that "a large employer of labour", obviously meaning Lewis, had sent his foremen to workers homes to instruct them, under threat of losing their jobs, to withdraw their children from the church school, a claim hotly denied in the local press. Conversely, the non-sectarians alleged that a child dying in an unlit room in Seymour Street was refused baptism by the Reverend Mortimer as the father was a supporter of the Educational League. Mr. Arthur Baines, the secretary of the local Amalgamated Society of Railway Workers was present and said that after seeing the child the priest remarked that he would not baptise the child until he had fetched his gown. It was 35 minutes later that the clergyman returned, by which time the child had died. He then refused to bury the infant as it was unbaptised.

By the September many parents were withdrawing their children from the school during religious education periods, as they were allowed to do under the Conscience Clause, over 300 being taken just round the corner to the Althorp Cafe for bible teaching. This was extremely disruptive and by October the register was being left open until 10 am as so many pupils were coming in late from instruction at the Cafe. In November something had to be done as discipline was fast breaking down and 48 boys were marked as absent as they were late arriving. On the 22nd of December all boys who attended the Cafe were sent home by order of the Church School managers.

Meanwhile, the church school extensions were being hurried on with all speed, in the hope that the relief from crowding would also provide a release from parent pressure. The new buildings were opened in December of 1898, but any hopes of a quieter New Year were forlorn.

The 9th of January 1899 saw the non-sectarian children arrive at school wearing medals struck by the St. James's Educational League, but they were removed upon the orders of the headmaster. The next day saw the Rev. Jabez Bell and Mr. Lewis patrolling the school gates encouraging boys to defy the head, and, when the youngsters refused to remove the badges in the school yard, there was a scene that was only resolved when the pupils were allowed to retain the badges until the actual moment that they entered the school buildings.

Three days later 300 "Cafe Boys" were refused admission to the school. A seething throng of pupils and furious parents outside the school premises created such an uproar that the police were sent for. Over 300 boys were turned away each day that week and St. James's End was on the verge of a riot. Rival schools were being set up, one at Doddridge Memorial Chapel and another in the St. James's Hall, with volunteer teachers. Court action was threatened when a small girl was caned for replacing her Educational League badge whilst in class.

It was obvious that the situation could not be tolerated for much longer by the authorities, and an explosive public inquiry was held at which all the grievances were aired. The veteran M.P. for Northampton, Henry Labouchiere, and the Liberal M.P. for South

The outcome of the row was the establishment of a Board School, known locally as the Tin School. Generations of pupils were taught here, like this class B5 in 1904.

Northants, Francis Channing, supported the Educational League, and the outcome was the decision to open another school in St. James's End, a Board School, non-sectarian and under the direct control of the local authority.

This turned out to be a crude corrugated-iron hut erected in the yard of the tram depot just across the road from the Church School. Such a distinctive construction became known, inevitably, to generations of Jimmy's End kids as The Tin School.

Eventually, this familiar landmark was superseded by the modern, verandahed board school in Lewis Road, opened in 1932 as Spencer School.

A Can-Tank-Erous Tale

This is the tale of Northampton's troublesome tank. It was trouble a-coming, controversial while it was here, and a problem going!

Many towns in the country ran savings schemes during the First World War, often called Tank Funds. After the war, when the army was disposing of its surplus armaments, unwanted tanks were commonly offered to towns where such funds had been raised. Northampton was offered one in recognition of it's notable efforts in the War Savings Campaign.

The corporation proudly accepted and the monster duly arrived at the Castle Station on Friday 24th of October, 1919. Monster it certainly was, for it was one of the largest tanks to see service, and was said to weigh over 20 tons. A civic christening service to dub it Steelback in honour of the Northants Regiment was arranged for the following Thursday allowing, it was thought, ample time to take the thing to Abington Park and set it up amid the trees alongside several field guns and cannons dating from earlier campaigns which already resided there.

Two army engineers accompanied the tank but, despite their strenuous efforts, the machine stubbornly refused to start. They couldn't even drive it off the railway wagon. A week later it was still there, much to the surprise and annoyance of councillors, for, earlier

The tank in Abington Park.

in the year when they had requested earlier delivery of the tank, the authorities had refused, on the grounds that, before being sent to the provinces, the vehicles were to be thoroughly overhauled.

The day of the civic ceremony arrived. Councillors, aldermen and distinguished guests assembled at Abington Park. The mayor, Councillor. J.J. Martin, rushed to the station hoping for a last minute thunder of engines, but all was still and quiet on this western front. Dejectedly, he returned to Abington Park to cancel the event.

It was on the following Saturday that the tank was eventually started and driven to the Market Square, where it again refused to start. It took a whole day to persuade it to move and it was Sunday when it left to pass up Billing Road on it's way to Abington. Yet again it expired, appropriately, this time, outside the gates of Billing Road Cemetery!

On Monday it finally arrived at Abington Park where it took up uneasy residence. Described by old Tank Corps men as a "male" tank as it had cannons in the side turrets rather than the machine guns of a "female" tank, it became a source of great irritation to many. Park-keepers hated it because children clambered down inside it and defied authority, while many folk felt that it was a glorification of war to have it there at all.

By 1934 the ripples still hadn't subsided and agitation to have the tank removed was getting stronger, whipped up by the Society of Friends, the Quakers, who organised a petition for its scrapping.

Councillor Barratt, in council, said that its presence aroused an interest in war and created a war mind in youngsters. He would only agree to the weapon's continued presence, he said, if photographs of terrible wounds inflicted by guns and tanks were attached so that they would serve a useful purpose as a warning. Alderman Collier, on the other hand, said that Northampton men who went out and fought for their country realised better than Councillor Barratt what they were fighting for and "though an ugly sight to the councillor, they were not an ugly sight in the lanes and streets of France when Tommies were glad to hear their cheerful response to the enemy".

After much discussion and heated argument the decision to remove the tank was taken by 24 votes to 12 in the early summer of 1934. A 'hornet's nest' of British Legion members, ex-servicemen organisations, and others descended on the councillors. "An insult to the memory of the dead" .... "It is just as logical to get rid of the Mobb's Memorial"......"They'll be getting rid of the ancient flintlock pistols from the museum, next!"

As the year rolled by into winter the guns and the tank were still there. The problem seemed to be what to do with them, particularly the tank with it's 20 tons of rusting steel. Mr. W. Care, vice president of the Northants British Legion, suggested removal to a better site. Councillor Barratt suggested that if Mr. Care was so keen on it, he should find a home for it. In a reply hinting at the councillor's profits from making army boots during the war, Mr. Care said, "I should be only too pleased to do so, but, as I served my country for four and a half years, it was not possible for me to acquire a mansion!"

One ingenious suggestion came from a local vicar. With heavy irony he advocated that it should be thrown open to souvenir hunters. "Speaking from experience", he said, "a fortnight should be long enough to dispose of a small thing like a tank!"

Mr. S.D. Bateman of the Castle Ward Conservative Men's Association proposed that the tank could be loaned to their Association so that they could blast the "green monstrosities" on the Mayorhold and Campbell Square, referring to the oval cast-iron urinals there.

Councillor Barratt retired from office, the New Year arrived, and still the tank sat in Abington Park. The lighter guns, of which there were five, were towed away on January the 7th, 1935. Three captured German field guns and two dating from the Boer War were hitched in a "train" behind a corporation steam lorry for their last trip to the West Bridge depot. A separate trip was needed for the three ton naval gun and it's huge, but rotten, wooden carriage.

The array of artillery pieces that were scrapped at the same time as the tank.

The Borough Engineer Mr. R.A. Winfield was left with the tank. It was suggested, in council, that a large hole be dug for it and it should be buried. Persistent local legend says that this was done, and that the monster still sleeps beneath the mound of earth near the bandstand in Abington Park. Not true, I'm afraid.

On the 6th February, 1935, John Shimeld from Sheffield and his mate arrived with their oxyacetylene cutting torches and set about slicing the tank up. Every bit was taken away for scrap; "Probably end up as razor blades", he told the local paper. Care was taken, however, not to destroy the bronze name plate with it's inscription as it was to be preserved .... I wonder what became of that? Is it still acting as a doorstop or a paper-weight in some borough office, do you think?

A Macabre Murder At Guilsborough

If you are of a squeamish disposition read no further, for today's tale is a gory story of murder most foul and a remorseful ghost.

John Croxford was a tailor at Brixworth, a small but ancient village six miles from Northampton on the coach-road north, and, by all accounts, an idle fellow who preferred poaching, gaming and drinking to following his trade. Like attracts like, they say, and Croxford had as his companions two lads from the nearby village of Guilsborough, Thomas Seamark, a shepherd, and Richard Butlin a breeches maker, and Benjamin Deacon, a carpenter from adjacent Spratton. None was over 30 years of age, and the combined age of all four was only 77 years.

Their minor depredations in neighbouring parishes soon, however, took a more ambitious turn and they commenced a career as footpads, robbing travellers on the turnpikes north from Northampton.

Some time between Michaelmas and St. Luke's Day, that is in the early part of October, in the year 1763, the four men were drinking in Seamark's shepherd hut on Catslo Grounds, to the south of Guilsborough, when a knock came on the door. Answering it, they found a travelling pedlar selling stockings, cloth and buttons. No, they said, they did not wish to buy anything. The pedlar left. Not loathe to seize an opportunity, the gang slipped out and a short way down the road, set upon the man.

He was a strong fellow and overpowering him was not easy, it took all of them to subdue him and drag him back into the yard of the house. Croxford and Deacon were first into the attack, Butlin holding back as it was his first such crime, and Seamark keeping watch. Still unable to control the pedlar they all piled on the man, Butlin laying on the legs, Deacon holding his thighs and hips, and Seamark his chest and arms. Croxford, meanwhile, seized a white hafted knife belonging to Seamark and slit the pedlars throat.

The body was stripped of clothes and the contents of the pockets, as well as the man's meagre wares, shared between the robbers. The corpse was buried in a nearby cucumber bed. Shortly after, however, when it was learned that the patch was soon to be ploughed, and knowing that the body would surely be discovered, they decided to dig it up again. An agitated discussion now took place as to how they should dispose of the body. One idea was to take it to a stack of bracken collected from the nearby heath and set fire to it. The inclement weather, though, put paid to that.

They settled, then, on cutting the body into manageable pieces and burning each piece on the open fire on Seamark's hearth. So the corpse was dismembered. Limbs were thrown upon the fire. The heart and stomach were thrown to the two dogs, one Seamark's and the other Deacon's, who fought for the titbits, tearing them apart. The intestines were tossed into the pigsty where the hog dragged them about before consuming them. The hearth was not big enough alone to burn the large quantity of flesh, so the attached oven was also utilised to destroy the arms.

The remaining bones were taken by the villains into the garden and pulverised with hammers until they were almost dust, when they were mixed with the ashes and buried beneath a lean-to hovel in the garden.

Mrs. Seamark had, of course, witnessed all of this, but was thought by the men to be no danger, as a wife could not be made to give evidence against her husband. What they did not know, though, was that Seamark's boy, Richard, not quite ten years old, had been wakened by the commotion and, leaving his upstairs bed, had witnessed the entire grisly scene through a crack in the floorboards.

The boy had already been in trouble, for he had seen the original killing of the pedlar. The day after the murder, and before the body was exhumed, he had said to his brothers, "If you give me a marble, I'll show you where Daddy and Croxford killed the man and buried him in the cucumber bed". In return he had taken them to the spot where they all saw wet blood still staining the grass. Horrified when they heard of it, the murderers threatened Richard with death should he ever breathe a word of what he had seen.

Some time after this episode, young Richard, being tormented by his fellow pupils at school, threatened, "I'll do to you what my father did to the pedlar. I'll put you in the oven!" Word soon got around and, before long, came to the ears of John Bateman of Guilsborough, the local J.P. Gathering together another local squire, Mr. Adcock, and a party of farmers, they went to the Seamark hovel where they interrogated Anne Seamark, who soon revealed the place where the ashes were buried, and the men recovered the powder and a few bones.

As it happened Anne Seamark was, by now, a widow. Some time had elapsed and her husband Thomas had gone on to commit highway robbery on his own account, had been caught, convicted at the Lent Assizes on the 6th March 1764 of robbing Thomas Quartley of Wicken of 30/- in silver and a silver watch, and sentenced to hang. He made no confession of his confederates and was carried, it was said, almost dead from fear, to his hanging.

John Croxford and Ben Deacon were already languishing in the County Gaol, having been arrested on 27th April 1764 and committed on suspicion of "divers felonies and robberies".

Richard Butlin, though, was captured almost coincidentally, when the constable of Brixworth went to premises at Nortoft, in Guilsborough, called The Hare, where the Butlin family lived, to arrest Joseph his brother for a quite different crime. His mother Jane, set about the officer, aided by Richard and uncle John Butlin, allowing Joseph to escape. A £40 reward was offered for his capture, effected soon after, in fact, at Brackley. John Butlin was sentenced to one months imprisonment for the episode, Jane to one week, while Richard was soon recognised as one of Croxford's murderous confederates and held for trial on more serious charges.

The trio was arraigned on the 2nd August, 1764, before Sir Thomas Parker, Lord Chief Baron of His Majesty's Court of Exchequer. The prosecution, led by Northampton Recorder Mr. Caldecott and another Kings Council, Mr. Mundy, first called Anne Seamark. With her husband dead and the other villains in gaol, she was an exemplary witness, composed, sincere and even-tempered; behaviour that was seen as the strongest proof of her innocence. She described the murder scene in ghastly detail.

The son, Richard Seamark, went into even more horrific particulars, recalling that when the pedlar's leg was on the fire, he saw the toes flicking between the flames and lying between other "hunks of meat" on the hearth. He also observed a man's hand sticking out of the oven.

Of the three defendants, only Butlin engaged council, the others defending themselves, and always proclaiming, loud and long, their total innocence. Their declarations were so strong and solemn, indeed, inviting the heaviest of penalties that God could inflict if they were guilty, that many of the crowd were persuaded of their blamelessness, and even more doubted.

Nevertheless, the jury withdrew, returning only 10 to 15 minutes later to pronounce the men "Guilty of committing a murder upon the body of a Person Unknown".

The prisoners seemed less affected by the verdict than the bystanders, as the time of the execution was set for two days hence, the 4th August 1764.

Still they all protested their innocence, and many locals believed them, so much so that it was feared that a rescue attempt might be made, so a party of General Sir Charles Howard's Regiment of Dragoons with bayonets fixed to their muskets and guns loaded with powder and ball, were engaged to escort the prisoners from the gaol to the place of execution.

As ringleader, Croxford's body was taken, after the hanging, to the crossroads on Hollowell Heath, not far from where the crime was committed, and hung in chains from the gibbet there. The bodies of the other two were given to surgeons for dissection, poetic justice, one might say.

Now that may well have been the end of the whole gruesome affair, but on Sunday the 12th August, 1764, a local parson was sitting in his study after the evening service, when he was surprised by the figure of a man standing just inside the door. Surprised because the door was securely locked from inside by a sturdy spring bolt. The man, observing the reverends dismay, told him to compose himself as he was there by the command of a Superior Power, and could thus do no-one any harm. He said that he was one of the unhappy prisoners that had been executed at Northampton a little over a week ago, and that, as he was the principal and leader of the gang, most of whom he had corrupted and debauched, he had been appointed by Providence to tell the world the truth.

The parson asked the apparition's name. John Croxford, was the reply. Why did the trio persist in their protestations of innocence, even on the scaffold? Well, said the figure, they had entered into a "sacramental obligation by dipping their fingers into the murdered man's blood and licking them, swearing under penalty of eternal damnation never to betray the fact of their crime, or to confess on the evidence of others."

The ghost also confirmed that all the details of the evidence were true. Did he know who the victim was? No, but he was a Scotchman, said Croxford. This was all very well, then said the parson, but it was an age when men were not at all disposed to believe visions or ghosts, and that the world would consider him mad or an impostor, so he would require some authentication of what the spectre was telling him.

Croxford, after a pause, then told of a gold ring, hacked from the fingers of the dead pedlar's hand. When examined as part of the spoils, the villains had noticed that it had an inscription inside it, reading *HANGED HE'LL BE, WHO STEALS ME. 1745*. All four being of a superstitious nature, none of them would have the ring, so it was buried in the parish of Guilsborough, at a spot described in minute detail by Croxford's ghost As darkness was by now falling, the parson opened the door to call for candles and, upon turning back, found that the ghost had disappeared.

Just after dawn the next morning, between four and five o'clock, the reverend set off to find the location of the ring and, sure enough, shallow digging revealed it, tallying exactly. with the ghost's description.

A tall story, garnished with theatrical detail? No, every single element is documented in court reports and local papers of the time, which only goes to prove that truth is at least as strange as fiction.

Jumbo Skulls At Cotton End

A stranger leaving town via Bridge Street, just a few decades ago, would have been surprised to be confronted by a couple of giant skulls as he traversed the railway level crossing. Locals, of course, were accustomed to the rather bizarre sight; indeed, they were, in a strange way, rather fond of the two great elephant skulls that rested on a specially constructed shelf and overlooked the roadway.

How they came to be there is an interesting tale. They did not both arrive at the same time, the first one was installed in 1927. At this time the Robert Fossett circus occupied land at Tiffield, as it did for many years, where many of the animals wintered after a strenuous season of travelling with the world famous show. Two of the more noticeable residents at this site were a pair of young elephants which had cost the circus the then very high price of £500 each.

In the October of 1927 one of the newly arrived elephants escaped from it's keeper, rampaged through the village trampling coops, scattering chickens and terrorising cottagers, before being captured by lamplight, as night fell, in a small backyard. The other animal, only eight years old and fresh from it's tropical homeland, was not made of such stern stuff and suffered badly from the English autumn, contracting pneumonia and dying soon after.

Called in to dispose of the body was well-known local horse slaughterer, Mr. John Tomkins, who lived just to the south-east of Bridge Street level crossing. While the rest of the carcase went the way of all flesh, so to speak, the skull was considered something of a curiosity, and so was displayed on a specially built shelf for the public to see .... a trade sign, you might say.

Mr. Tomkins had only recently moved from the vicinity of Winchester Street, in the town, where he had started his business, and had established his slaughterhouse in Hardingstone. The way he dealt with the dead elephant was obviously satisfactory (A dead elephant presents one big problem, it was pointed out to me by Mr. Tomkin's grandson. Alive it will negotiate a doorway; when dead it will not and often has to be dissected *in-situ* to remove it!) and from then on he dealt with all dead animals from Fossett's winter quarters. As well as elephants, he disposed of lions, bears, leopards, okapis, llamas, etc.

So it might have remained, a solitary young elephant's skull, had it not been for Aga. Aga was a giant, even by elephantine standards, weighing in at 4 tons 7½ cwts. She was performing with Hackenberg's Circus in Hamburg, one of Europe's premier circuses, when Robert Fossett senior first clapped eyes on her. He bought her from Hackenberg's in 1925. She was a natural performer, a brilliantly intelligent animal, patient and gentle, and a great favourite with children and adults alike. In 1936 she achieved stardom when the United Artist's film company decided to shoot a film called "Elephant Boy" with, in the lead, an Indian child actor being hailed as a great discovery, called Sabu. The original intention was to bring back a suitably trained elephant from India when the film crew returned from shooting the location sequences, but the expense and the difficulties of quarantine forced them to abandon the plan.

The answer was Aga. She travelled down to the Denham studios where she was fitted out with huge imitation tusks,(her own were too small for a film star!) and she acquired a stage name of Iravatha.

At the outbreak of war, in 1939, Aga as usual came to winter at Tiffield, but now she did war work, felling and shifting timber and even pulling a plough.

Aga the elephant as she appeared in the film "Elephant Boy" with Indian child actor Sabu.

As the winter drew in Aga took ill and almost immediately, died. Again Mr. Tomkins was called in to deal with the corpse, and another skull, this time a huge 57 year-old one, joined the young 8 year-old one on the shelf at Cotton End. Flanking them, too, were the giant thigh-bones of Aga.

For two decades the skulls were a landmark to all who travelled out of Northampton southwards. Though most local folk were not aware of it, the skulls were changed fairly frequently as they degenerated in the weather and were replaced as animals died.

The old white house at Cotton End, where Mr. Tomkins lived, with its stables alongside, were knocked down to make way for a more modern concrete structure with garages on the ground floor and living quarters above but a strong concrete shelf was incorporated to hold the skulls.

Around 1966, following the death of John Tomkins's son, the business was sold to a former employee (it still trades as Tomkins Slaughters, at Hanslope), the skulls were removed and the premises were used by a car repair firm. Eventually, the area was flattened, buildings and all, to make way for commercial developments, including the Co-op superstore. What happened to the skulls? I do not know, they disappeared without trace, probably just taken to the tip ..... a sad, but inevitable, end for Aga and her friend. But if you talk to almost any Northamptonian of an appropriate age they will remember the bizarre relics.

St. James's Abbey

Peverels Way, Abbotts Way, Abbey Street; just street names in St. James's End, but also the very last echoes of the powerful and important Abbey of St. James that once stood there and spread its influence throughout the county.

Back at the beginning of the 12th century a high-ranking Norman nobleman, William Peverel, whose story features in Sir Walter Scott's "Peverel of the Peak", founded a house for the Black Canons of Augustines well outside the western extremities of Northampton town. The buildings were of wood and were sited, as far as is known, where the Express Lifts factory stands today.

Endowed with 40 acres of land, the church at Duston, Duston Mill, and extensive free meadow rights, King Henry I confirmed the abbey's establishment in 1104. Rich benefactors added to the monks' wealth and before long the abbey owned property in 60 Northamptonshire parishes and rents in Rutland, Bedfordshire, and Leicestershire, as well as in the teeming slums of Charing Cross, London. Many churches were in their hands, too, at Duston, Bozeat, Weekley, Spratton, Rothersthorpe, Horton, Watford, and Litchborough, as well as farther afield in such places as Gaddesden Parva in Hertfordshire. They also held two moieties, shared privileges, at Roade and Hartwell, supplying the Cure of these parishes for two years out of every three. The value of this can be judged from the fact that they once held the moiety of Helmdon, but relinquished it to the Master of St. John's Hospital, in Northampton, in return for 20/- to be paid annually. When you consider that, in 1291, the annual income for St James's Abbey was £70. 0. 2d, and was among the wealthiest, the figure comes into sharp perspective.

The first Abbott was Ralph, who took up the post in 1158 (formerly the Abbey was probably run by a Prior) and he busily began to construct more permanent stone buildings. In the reign of Henry II, on 15th July 1173, to be exact, Ralph and his canons left the wooden buildings to occupy the new monastery and church of St. James.

Not long after, in the early years of the 13th century, fire seriously damaged the new abbey. The rebuilding was slow in being done, and in 1223 Henry III gave 30 huge oak rafters from his forest to speed the restoration. Even so, six years later the reconstruction had still not been finished and in 1229 the king sent an order to Stephen de Seagrave to grant the Abbott two more oaks from the Kings Park at Moulton to be used in building the tower.

The Abbott, at this time, was a powerful personage locally, and was entrusted by the King to enforce his edicts. Thus, in 1234, and again in 1236, when knights and noblemen planned to fight a tourney at Yardley Hastings without the King's express permission, the

Abbott was sent to enforce a royal ban on the proceedings.

Walter, the Abbott at this time, died in 1237. Two canons were sent to the King to inform him of the death and to seek permission to elect a successor. This the King gave on May 27th and one Adam Gilly, one of the St. James's canons was chosen. On 7th June the King approved the appointment and ordered the Bishop of Lincoln to "do his part therein". The Bishop, it seems, did not approve and quashed the election. By the end of June the canons were once more authorised to elect an Abbott. This time they selected their Prior, Osbert of Luffenham. The royal assent was given on 15th August and Osbert duly became Abbott. Perhaps controversy still rankled, we don't know, but five years on Osbert resigned, and the canons again elected Adam Gilly. The formalities, this time, were unopposed and he became Abbot.

Fairs were a great part of the medieval scene and St. James's was no exception. In 1268 the King granted licence to the Abbey to hold a fair each year in the Convent precincts on the eve of the festival of St. James and on the two following days. This was a useful source of revenue for the Abbey in the early times but, in later years, it sadly diminished until it barely covered expenses.

The Abbott, personally, was the recipient of lands and benefits that made him privately wealthy. At the end of the 13th century he is noted as renting 45 acres of land from Eustace de Watford for sixpence a year, a pound of pepper and a pound of cummin, valued at tenpence.

In the year 1290 all Jews were banished from England and their property seized by the King. The local monks were at the forefront of the persecution and were beneficiaries when the King redistributed much of the booty to religious houses. St. James's Abbey was given the Northampton Synagogue, a number of town houses that adjoined it, and several nearby buildings that had belonged to one Sarra de London, a rich jewess. The entire gift was valued at 14/8d, and in return the Canons had to pay the King a yearly sum of one penny and to pray for the soul of the monarch.

Nicholas de Flore became Abbott as the new century began, and he brought new ideas to the establishment. He began a monastic register and established an extensive library. Unfortunately, a disastrous fire at the Cottonian Library in 1731 destroyed many surviving documents from the Abbeys collection and the remains are now kept at the British Museum. By good luck, however, copies of some of the manuscripts were made in 1720 and these are now in the Bodleian Library at Oxford and are the source of much of our knowledge of the Abbey.

Not all the monks were dedicated, we find, for in 1309 one of the Canons, John de Horewood, was excommunicated for apostasy, the abandonment of religious orders. He ran away from the Abbey. He later returned in disgrace to do penance. John de Alkonbury behaved similarly in 1341.

Though the establishment's resources were running down, its influence remained, and a high spot in the Order's history came in 1318 when the Keeper of the Rolls of Chancery came to the Abbey bringing with him the Great Seal of England. There was, at this time, an inn that formed part of the monastery, and it was here that the Seal was delivered to the "chancellor" who took it from it's bag and sealed important writs with it. It remained at St.

James's for a month thereafter.

The following year Nicholas, the elderly Abbott, was summoned to Parliament. Being old and infirm he appointed his Canon of House, Henry de Blisworth, as proxy. Parliament, however, examined the Abbey records, observing that the Abbey was now severely impoverished and held only free alms from the King, decided that sending a Canon to London would be a great burden for so poor an order, so excused his presence.

Soon after, Nicholas de Flore died, having served as Abbott for 35 years. A tablet to his memory survived in Duston Church. Part of the lengthy and worn inscription described him as "the flower of Flower" (Flore).

As the importance of St. James's Abbey grew, administrative tasks were entrusted to the monks by Parliament. In 1340 Gerard de Combes, the then Abbott, was appointed tax collector for Northamptonshire. Because, in the words of Parliament, "certain Lords of towns and other parts were striving to defraud the King of the greater part of subsidy, granted in his urgent need for the defence of the realm", selected abbotts throughout the land were instructed to take every ninth fleece, ninth lamb, and ninth sheaf of corn in every parish, and, in cities and boroughs, to take a ninth of all goods in tax. The Abbott must have met with some resistance for, on 15th July of that year, a stern order was sent to him to arrest and imprison anyone impeding the collector. Similarly, if the collectors delayed delivery of the money they, likewise, would be punished.

This tax was eased four years later, first to one tenth and then to one fifteenth, and a special strong-room was ordered to be provided by the monks at St. James's Abbey to hold the money, and where the crown agents could have free access.

Even this did not relieve the King's impoverishment. Two years on, and his wars in France had drained the coffers. He had won the Battle of Crecy and was besieging Calais, and was desperately in need of more funds. A programme of compulsory loans from monasteries was instituted, the sum from each being based on the Order's assessed wealth. St. James's Abbey contributed £5. 6s. 8d which the King undertook to repay at Christmas 1348. This sum compared with £40 from the abbey at Peterborough, £11. 6s. 8d from Sulby, and £5. 13s. 4d from Canons Ashby and Daventry, which gives some idea of the local abbey's financial straits at this time.

Another burden suffered by the monks of St. James's was the sending by the King of pensioned-off servants and courtiers to be looked after in old age at the Abbey. One such was Ralph, one time Yoeman of the King's Napery, who lived a life of considerable comfort at the Abbey for several years. This custom went on, each pensioner being replaced as they died, until 1444 when the Abbott sought, and obtained, exemption, finally convincing Henry VI of the Order's poverty.

One of the most important areas of land owned by the Abbey was at Bozeat, where they let 180 acres to freemen. Each man's family had to fulfil specified annual tasks on the Canon's land and certain requirements in trade. They had to pay 20 pence yearly in rent, supply two hens to the Lord Abbott at Christmas, and 20 eggs at Easter. They also owed him 3 days ploughing a year, one in return for forage rights and two for ploughing rights. Those freemen without cattle fit for ploughing would give one penny instead. They also had to provide one day's weeding a year and general help for three days in the autumn (two days without a provided meal and one day with food at the Lord Abbott's table). Each had to carry the Lord's goods by wagon for one day a year, thresh his corn for one day, and collect nuts in the autumn for one day. Any colt sold for more than 5/- required that 4d had to be given to the Lord, any pig killed cost the freeman 1d if a year old, ½d if only six months. Colts and bulls could not be sold on the open market without first being offered to the Lord's bailiff. Even private life in the village was controlled by the Abbey. If a woman was unchaste she paid a fine to the Lord Abbott. If she happened to be a widow she was to be given in marriage at the Lord's will. These dues had to be performed by the entire family, with the exception of the mother.

The Abbey's religious reputation was widely known, and nobles and persons of importance left sums of money to ensure that they were buried within the precincts. Sir John Catesby, a Justice of Common Pleas, was buried here in 1485, as was Richard Woodville, Earl Rivers, the brother in law of Edward IV and uncle of Elizabeth, King Henry VII's queen. The Woodvilles had made an earlier, less auspicious, appearance in the Abbey's history when, in 1434, Thomas Woodville gave lands and property in his will to the Abbott and Convent, but his son Anthony, Earl Rivers, evicted the Canons and seized the land for himself. The Abbott appealed to the King and instructions were sent to the Sheriff of Northamptonshire to restore the property to the monks, by force if necessary.

Some gifts were made for other reasons, often to enable the faithful to undertake pilgrimages. To this end, for instance, Simon, son of Ralph Barre, gave his mill at Great Billing to the Canons in return for 40/- rent annually and a down payment of 70 marks to finance a journey to Jerusalem.

The order at St. James's got involved in King Henry VIII's row with the Roman Catholic church, too. In 1534 Abbott John Dassett and eight of his Canons signed, as they were required to do, the documents acknowledging Henry as head of the church and denying the authority of the Pope. Even so, two years later the King's commissioners arrived at St. James's Abbey with the intention of suppressing it. They sent back to London, however, a glowing report of the monks' work in the county. The Abbott was, they said, a discreet man who managed the abbey well. By his alms some eighty poor people were fed and comforted each day, though Northampton was a "towne of moche povertie and ympotent people". The King was not particularly impressed by this report, however. In fact, he suggested, loudly, and probably with some justification, that the commissioners had been bribed.

Just at this critical time Abbott Dassett died, and it seemed likely that the house would be suppressed. What probably saved the Abbey was the diplomatic appointment of one William Brockton, one of Cardinal Wolseley's lackeys, as Abbott Elect; that and the payment of the huge sum of £333. 6s. 8d.

The Convent Seal, the official authority to run the Abbey was, meanwhile, still retained by Thomas Cromwell, Wolseley's secretary, and he had fallen out with the new Abbott. Counter-pleas for the return of the Seal, on one hand, and for the arrest of Canons who campaigned against King's commissioners, on the other, made for bitter arguments and difficult relations, but in 1538 the seals of office were conveyed back to the Abbey. It was a hollow victory, though, for almost the first document to be sealed with them was the very deed of surrender that the monks had been fighting. The Abbey, all its houses, its inn, land and properties, were handed over to the King.

The Abbey site and some lands were acquired by one of the commissioners, George Gifford. He dismantled the Abbey buildings, using some of the stone to build himself a mansion on the land. The rest of the stone he sold locally or used in the construction of walls. Right into the last century many of the walls that divided the Six Fields could be seen to contain bits of old window and door surrounds. Indeed, a section of wall that is believed to have been an outer wall of the Abbey grounds was still in place alongside the Weedon Road, near the junction with Duston Road, as late as the 1920s.

What is thought to be the site of the Abbey church was found when the tennis courts were constructed at the front of the Express Lifts factory, and the finding of graves and stone coffins when digging the footings of the present offices suggests that as the site of the graveyard. Some relics were found, too, a two-handled drinking cup, several coins, and a stone coffin, but all too little to tell us much of the life-style of the Black Canons of St. James's Abbey.

The Boy O'Bell Barn

With his fringe of white hair atop a large and bushy snow-white beard, Charles Wright was a patrician figure around Northampton just after the turn of the century.
Born in 1830, he was known throughout the county as the "Boy o' Bell Barn" after the place where he was born. Bell Barn was an area of Victorian slums surrounding St. Andrew's Church and tumbling down the hill side to meet the notorious "Boroughs".

By his own account, Charles Wright was a precocious lad, getting into all sorts of mischief before being sent away to Bedford and attending Dr. Riley's Preparatory School. He soon developed a talent for writing plays and became fascinated by the theatre. Returning to Northampton he found himself drawn to the stage, getting odd jobs at an old theatre that used to stand on the corner of Marefair and Horseshoe Street.

One day he was passing down Newland when he heard the sound of singing coming from the New Hall, later called the Milton Hall. Entering at the back, he found himself in a meeting of the Mutual Improvement Society. Suddenly, the chairman called on him to contribute, which he did by giving an impromptu dramatic recitation, a performance that was met with great acclaim and an invitation to join a concert party.

As a result of this baptism of fire he gravitated to London where he was in great demand as a writer of dramas, sketches and songs, his pantomime "books" being particularly popular. As his wealth increased he turned to theatre management, opening no fewer than seven music halls in and around London, among them the famous Elephant and Castle Music Hall.

In his fame, however, he did not forget his early hardships and a dramatic poem called "The Life of a Comic Singer" was a great favourite in the profession, where it echoed many a stars humble beginnings.

Suddenly, though, the "Boy o' Bell Barn", by now his pen-name, left the stage to take a job as head waiter at the Stock Exchange. He became something of a "character" with wealth and position. Twice he had the honour of sitting at table with King Edward VII.

Then he "got religion", as the saying goes. He became an evangelist. For thirty years he was a familiar figure at Epsom race course where he conducted mission meetings on big race days. Returning to his native town, he opened a mission hall in Bath Street, with a refreshment room attached to it which he manned himself, still writing poems and ballads meanwhile under his pseudonym.

In politics he was, like most Northamptonians at that time, a Liberal, and he composed many songs in their support.

He had been married in 1852, and he and his wife retired to Kingsthorpe where they lived out the rest of their lives, the "Boy o' Bell Barn" with his long white whiskers and Victorian clothes becoming a much-loved and familiar figure.

The "Boy o'Bell Barn" in later years.

Some County Characters

There were many quaint characters around years ago and, sadly, in a robust age, they were often the butt of cruel jokes and taunts. It is nice, then, to hear of one such character who had the last laugh.

O'Connor was a rag and bone man, just after the turn of the century, and as his name would indicate, was of Irish extraction. He was the butt of the local children as his thick Irish brogue made his speech almost unintelligible, and his street-cry a thunderous gabble that could have been interpreted as almost anything. Because of this he was treated as something of a simpleton. He was however, quietly making money and salting it away. Imagine, then, the amazement of the locals when, one day, he upped and bought a large old malthouse in Marefair and transformed it into a tasteful three storey house!

Another rag and bone man of the same era was one Billy Leek of Harpole. His street-cry was shrill and piercing, the result, it was said, of his being found guilty of crime by the court and hung on the gallows for an hour before being cut down, found to be still alive, and freed. The local children sang a couplet that included the lines:-

Billy Leek of Harpole,
Lay on the ground to watch the grass grow.

A familiar sight in the south of the county, at the end of the last century, was a curious couple of men, inseparable friends, who had only one leg between them. Samuel Keyves was the owner of the real leg, and was a cleaner at Wolverton's market hall. In his distinctive dress of stove-pipe hat, moleskin trousers, and with a spotted kerchief about his

Sam Keyves, on the left, and Sam Kendall, on right, two south Northants. characters with only one leg between them!

neck, he also made himself useful sweeping gutters. His friend Samuel Kendall had two wooden legs and an even stranger claim to notoriety. He was buried in two places! Employed as an engine driver on the London, North Western Railway, he met with an accident on the line at Castlethorpe which severed both his legs. These were buried in Castlethorpe churchyard, his body eventually being interred in the churchyard of St. George's church at Wolverton upon his death.

Another character was "Old Poppett" who sprinkled Northampton streets. He lived in a little hut in the grounds of Vigo gardens, the area between Billing Road and Bedford Road, before any houses were built in that area. In the days when dirt roads were liberally laced with horse manure, traffic raised great clouds of dust in the summer. Old Poppett was employed by the corporation as a roadman and to fetch and carry water from the pumps at Jeyes Jetty, Swan Yard and Wood Hill. He had facial

Old Poppett, the Northampton water carrier.

features that were not unlike the Duke of Wellington and his attire usually consisted of faded corduroy breeches of an antique cut, a buckskin waistcoat, and a swallow-tailed coat of long-forgotten style, topped off with a stove-pipe beaver hat. His notable physical feature, however, was his extremely bowed legs between which he would carry a large watering can suspended from a strap around his neck, with which he sprinkled the roads to keep the dust down.

Woodford, near Thrapston, produced two characters worthy of mention here. Simon Eady was a startling figure as he wandered the lanes thereabouts. A short, powerful man, he had long tangled locks which mingled with a shaggy beard. On his head he wore a hat described as "like a panchion". His clothing was made of rags and papers, these being cut and overlapped in such a way that they had all the appearance of scales. Over the lot was flung, rather flamboyantly, a tattered cloak.

From the same village came a man of greater note, an athlete of some prowess. Josiah Eaton was his name and he was a champion pedestrian, a marathon walker. With a national reputation, he performed an extraordinary feat in 1818 at Stowmarket. Here he started at 2 pm on the 12th May to walk for six weeks, covering a quarter of a mile in every successive quarter of an hour, finishing on the 3rd June. Among his earlier achievements were walking 2,000 miles in 42 days at Wormwood Scrubs in 1817, walking from Colchester to London in one day, returning the next day, and then repeating this for 20 successive days, a total of 1,020 miles, in September of 1817. At Brixton Causeway, in 1816, he covered 1,998 half miles in 1,998 successive half hours. Like his fellow Woodfordian Eady, Eaton was a short man, being only 5'2" tall.

Underneath the portico of All Saints Church, Northampton, used to be a monument to an ancient man. John Bailes was his name and he was buried here in 1706. His age was variously reported as 126, 114, or even 130 years old. Bailes claimed the latter figure. Certainly, he was a great age. Bailes earned a living as a button maker, hammering out discs of metal with small wooden dies, and joining them to bases and shanks. His age at death is now impossible to determine accurately, but he himself used to say that he was present at Tilbury Camp when Queen Elizabeth I reviewed the troops gathered to repel the Spanish invasion of 1588, and to prove it would quote details such as only an eyewitness could know. He said that he was twelve years old at the time, which would make him 130 years old at his death. His daughter, who survived him, said that she, herself, was 102 years old when he died. There is no register old enough to record his baptism, so the legend of his old age can now never be proved or disproved. After his death his frail body was dissected by local medical men in an attempt to discover the secret of his longevity, and the results published by Dr. James Keill in "Philosophical Transactions" of April 1706. He, too, was small of stature, with a large chest, fibrous heart, and strong lungs.

These were just a few of Northamptonshire's quaint catalogue of characters. Many more could be listed, "Old Moore", "Noddling Tommy", "Old Tommy No Legs", "Tommy Touch Corner", "Old Billy Orams", to name but five......

The Kingsthorpe Coal Mine

In view of Mr Scargill's recent support for lost causes, perhaps someone will direct his attention to the great Kingsthorpe coalmines and what is described in print as "the great national importance of Kingsthorpe coal fields".

In the early decades of the last century a group of Northampton business men floated a company, the Northampton Great Central Coal Mining Company, with the intention of recovering coal from a site at the top of Boughton Green Road. With a declared capital of £21,500 in £1 shares, the money was raised largely from small investments by local people.

A committee of management was set up with two secretaries and nine prominent local men. Joseph Adnitt a merchant of Bridge Street, headed the group, with William Butcher a gentleman of Hardingstone, John Duley an ironfounder of St. John's Street, John Lillyman a brushmaker, Robert Mills a clothier, Spence Jones a shoemaker, William Dunkley a farmer, William Roe a gentleman, and town alderman Mr William Porter of St. Andrew's Terrace, making up the committee.

The prospectus was tempting. "The period has arrived", it said, "when a combination of fortuitous and most advantageous circumstances have enhanced the importance so long attached to the discovery of coal", and continued by extolling the "great national importance of the Kingsthorpe coal fields".

In 1836 a shaft was drilled amid a local fever of speculation. At a depth of 210 feet the drill entered a strata of limestone and shortly after struck spring water. This was said to have been of almost spa quality and flowed at the rate of some 36,000 gallons per hour. Pressing on, the drill hit more water at 880 feet, this time a brackish supply. At 1,000 feet the workers had still not found coal and drilling was abandoned, though, significantly, the fact was not made public.

Then, surprise, rumour swept the town that coal had at last been found. Shareholders and local newspaper reporters, trying to confirm the stories, found that the company's engineer "was not available for comment", indeed, he could not be found. Folk who knew about these things soon realised that there was something odd about all of this, and it was not long before a written statement by the engineer was discovered stating that pieces of coal had been found in the shaft ..... but that he had put them there himself! It seemed that some among those running the company had arranged for the mine to be "salted", that is, planted with coal, in an attempt to increase the value of shares so that they could be disposed of at a profit. The engineer added that, in his opinion, there was no coal within miles of the site.

A row of cottages, called locally Coalpit Cottages, and a derelict chimney marked

The brow of the hill on Boughton Green Road where, just beyond the windmill, was the site of the infamous "coalmine".

the abandoned site for many years, though all traces now seem to have disappeared. The coalmines still live on in local legend, however, with lots of natives being able to point "authoritatively" to the site of the shaft.

Sweet Adeline of Deene

Deene House

At Deene Park, the ancient home of the Brudenells, just the other side of Kettering, there are rows of portraits with dignified faces gazing out aloofly over the many visitors to the house, and you can sense the almost tangible presence of the great 7th Earl of Cardigan, hero of Balaklava. Yet, there is one painting that stops you in your tracks. A stunning, dark haired, doe-eyed beauty with a sensual mouth, wearing a blue silk dress covered with black lace, a red rose in her hair and another perched provocatively in her corsage. It is Adeline de Horsey, one-time mistress of the 7th Earl and later his second wife.

Adeline was born in 1824, the daughter of Admiral Spencer de Horsey and his wife Louisa. As she reached her teens she blossomed into one of the most beautiful women of her day with a fine figure and elegant legs. She was well educated in the manner of the time, able to speak five languages and play the piano well. She also had a fine voice which she used to advantage when entertaining her parents guest's. She even wrote a complete opera score when she was a mere fifteen.

A portrait that hangs in Deene, and that illustrates Adeline's stunning beauty.

In 1842, when Adeline was 17, she appeared at court for her "coming out". Three years later she attended court again for a fancy dress ball at which the Earl of Cardigan, already a popular hero as the leader of the Charge of the Light Brigade, appeared dressed dashingly as an 18th century Dragoon. Significantly, soon after this, Adeline and her mother Louisa visited Deene.

The following year her mother died and a controlling influence went out of her life. Her Admiral father's rakish ways and frequent absences left her to run wild and indulge her fiery temper.

At 25 she became engaged to Count Montemolin, a pretender to the Spanish throne, but she soon broke that off as she became disenchanted by his hopeless pursuit of the crown.

Now, a wayward and uncontrollable young woman, she figuratively threw her cap into the social arena and moved with the fast set that included the famous courtesan Skittles. The two were great friends and used to ride the Quorn country together, Skittles often referring to Adeline as "the head of our profession".

Adeline's path crossed Cardigan's again in the January of 1857 when she went to a house party at Deene. Now, her impact on the 60 year-old Earl, who had been separated from Elizabeth his wife for some years, was noticeably different. From treating her like a wayward child, he now plainly saw her as a luscious woman and was obviously smitten. The open enmity of others like Lady Villiers and the Duchess of Montrose, who were vying for his favours, confirmed that his attentions had not gone un-noticed.

James, the 7th Earl of Cardigan, had had a turbulent life. He had eloped with Elizabeth Tollemache, a fellow officer's wife, and had become embroiled in a very messy divorce case. He had suffered a criminal suite over his adultery with Lady Francis Paget. The young wife of Sir William Leeson had run off with Cardigan and died aboard his yacht, and he had fought several duels, killing one man. Cardigan had known Admiral de Horsey, Adeline's father, for some time before the Crimea and had both sailed from the Royal Yacht Squadron at Cowes.

Upon Adeline's return to London Cardigan promptly followed, wooing her so vigorously and openly that it soon became the subject of society gossip. Word rapidly got back to the Admiral who banished his daughter to her quarters and forbade her to meet Cardigan, threatening to remove her to the country. Ever resourceful, she devised a method of suspending love notes from a line over the street, which Cardigan would collect as he rode by, re-attaching his missives for reeling in by her.

Being financially independent and having private means, she resolved to leave her father's house in Upper Grosvenor Street, taking up rooms in an hotel whilst Cardigan was preparing a love nest just off Park Lane. Very shortly she was installed there as the 7th Earl's mistress.

This was not, however, a hole and corner affair. They rode together in fashionable Rotten Row in great style, he a handsome figure in military style clothes, she in brightly coloured riding habits of silk and velvet with large brimmed, luxuriously feathered, hats.

For 18 months they lived together, looked after by four house-servants until, early in the morning on 12th July 1858, Adeline was awakened by Cardigan banging on the door. He had ridden furiously to the house to tell her excitedly that his wife, Elizabeth, Countess of Cardigan, had died. Following the deathbed wishes of Elizabeth, he proposed marriage, right away, to Adeline.

A sculptured bust of Adeline that was considered daring in its day, with the rose peeping from her cleavage.

Oddly, considering her scorn of conventions, she refused to marry Cardigan at once, sending him off to Ireland for a decent period of mourning.

In September of 1858 she joined Cardigan on his yacht "Airedale" at Cowes, sailing off with a full boat load of friends to Gibraltar, where they were married in the regimental church on the Rock.

Controversy and the ostracism which they had suffered in English society did not escape them, even there. The Governor of Gibraltar sent an invitation to dinner to Cardigan alone. He replied that he was in Gibraltar with his wife Lady Cardigan. Back came the invitation again, pointedly a single invite. Cardigan responded with a challenge to a duel. The Governor wisely ignored this, but had the Airedale towed out of the harbour and cut loose at sea.

However, they were honoured elsewhere in their honeymoon travels, places like Madrid, where they were guests of honour at Queen Isabella's birthday parade. Surprisingly, in view of the scandal occasioned by their living so publicly together, they were also granted an audience by Pope Pius IX and travelled triumphantly through Rome to the Vatican in a six-horse coach with an escort of Papal Guards.

Returning to England by way of Paris, they arrived back at Deene Park to be accompanied from the railway station to their estates by a 600-strong mounted escort of tenants.

In England, society and the aristocracy continued to shun the couple. It was apparently acceptable for the nobility to have lovers and mistresses, but not to marry them! Adeline immediately made her presence felt upon the scene. She appeared prominently in the Peeresse's Gallery of the House of Lords, to which she now had a traditional right. Both she and Cardigan rode to hounds with the Quorn and the Pytchley, but it was Adeline who was the dashing thruster, earning a reputation as the best horsewoman in those counties.

Cardigan was still enthraled with his Adeline, even though the match was not totally idyllic. He would not allow any other man to escort her into dinner, which was plainly absurd at a house party. She had a fiery temper and often threw plates at him and the servants. He had flirtations, too, "entertaining" ladies in the summerhouses around the estate, thinking that Adeline was unaware, but in later years she declared that she had known, but had allowed such dalliance as long as it was discreet.

Cardigan was still invited, as a national hero, to balls and formal occasions at Buckingham Palace, though Queen Victoria strongly disapproved of his presence. A painting exists showing Cardigan describing the great Charge of the Light Brigade to the royal family. The Queen was supposedly included in the group when the picture was first executed, but insisted on being painted out when she learned about the Earl's lifestyle! Enough was enough, however, and because he still adored Adeline he decided, before long, that he would go nowhere unless she was accepted also.

At the age of 71 Cardigan still insisted that his carriage was driven at breakneck speed wherever it took him, and he probably rode his horse in the same way. On 26th March 1868 he had an accident on the road between Deene and Gretton and two days later he died. To the great sadness of both Cardigan and Adeline, they had no children. He was the last of the direct line of Brudenells.

Being childless, the title passed to second cousin the Marquess of Ailesbury, but Adeline continued to live at Deene. After an appropriate period of mourning she returned to the extravagant circle of the Prince of Wales, the Marquess of Queensbury and the famous courtesans of the day as a very merry widow.

After a series of "amores", and despite having received a dozen or more proposals of marriage in the meantime, her eyes alighted, in 1872, on the politician Benjamin Disraeli. His wife had died that year and Adeline probably thought that marriage to him would give her the access to the court which her scandalous living with Cardigan had denied her.

She hunted him relentlessly. She invited him to Deene. She wrote him passionate and indiscreet love letters. On St. Valentine's Day 1873 she sent him a little white bust of herself. She even proposed to him. She finally tried a *fait accompli* by naming the day of their wedding! The vigour of her attack, however, as is often the way, frightened him off, especially since the matter, was becoming public knowledge and arousing much gossip. Queen Victoria, if it came to her ears, would certainly not have approved, so he fled from her advances.

She found consolation in 1873 by marrying a Portuguese nobleman, Count de

Lancastre. It was not a successful partnership, he was overshadowed by her strong personality and, although they were separated after six turbulent years, the marriage survived until his death in 1898.

She became a strident and autocratic character, a byword for eccentricity. Deene became run down, the servants often drunk. She smoked cigarettes both in public and private in an age when that alone would shock visitors.

Adeline took to bicycling around the grounds and nearby lanes wearing the 7th Earl's red-trousered "cherry-bum" uniform which he had worn at the famous Charge of the Light Brigade and which she referred to as her bicycling costume.

This, once more, brought her into conflict with the aging Queen Victoria. Adeline's title since her latest marriage, was The Countess of Cardigan and Lancaster. Queen Victoria, on her travels incognito to the spas of Europe, often used the pseudonym of the Countess of Lancaster. The titles were so similar that a story got back to the Queen that the monarch had been seen wearing pink tights and smoking a cigarette, riding a bike! She was not amused!

Adeline loved to shock and would often appear in Hyde Park in a gold wig, tricorn hat and elaborately embroidered coat, with a leopard skin thrown over her shoulders like a cloak, on the arm of an elderly escort. Following would be one of her footmen carrying her pet dog on a cushion.

Despite everything, she had style. She still rode about in a fine carriage with postilions uniformed in red jackets, white breeches and top boots, and footmen standing at the rear. Footmen in the house were all six foot plus and wore black tail-coats with crested silver buttons, scarlet breeches, white stockings and buckled shoes. In an age when such things had largely disappeared, they still had to wear powdered wigs.

Though now old and unable to ride, she refused to admit it and still went to the meets of the hunt, dressed in her riding outfit, but in a carriage. She would wait until the field was about to move off, then swear about her groom who had, she said, failed to turn up with her horses. She would then return home.

In the 1890s she scandalised the village by coming out shooting dressed in highland dress which revealed her knees.

She became convinced that Deene Park was haunted and told everyone so. She used to dress in flowing, ghostly white robes and dart around the house scaring guests and servants. She once appeared in the Great Hall, darkened deliberately, during a house party dressed as a white nun and singing Ave Maria. One lady was so terrified, she fainted!

In the house she kept her coffin, a quality product made to her own design in Oundle. Often she would have it carried into the Hall, put on her favourite old blue silk dress and lay back in the coffin asking onlookers how she looked. Her age made it difficult for her to get out again, so she had to call for assistance from the servants to extricate her.

For a while she still went to stay on her yacht The Seahorse, in Cowes Regatta week, and would be rowed about the harbour in her gig while she sang and played Italian serenades on her guitar.

As the century turned she lived at Deene surrounded by pet dogs, becoming increasing irascible and eccentric. She would often appear wearing the robes of a peeress, her face plastered in heavy make-up to hide the wrinkles and with a curly yellow wig in which was thrust an artificial rose. On one occasion, it was said, a guest arrived late for dinner. Adeline had already given his meat to her dogs, though they had not yet eaten it. She recovered the morsel, dusted it off, returning it to the dish, from where the guest took it and ate it.

Occasionally her past affairs would arise from the past to remind her. She had often said, in her younger days, that there were only two kinds of men guests. Those kind ones who, when she knocked on their bedroom doors, let her in, and those unkind ones who kept quiet. Mr Leveson-Gower was one of the latter and, when invited to Deene fifty years later was confronted by Adeline who drew his attention to a revealing bust of herself. Tapping the breasts with her fan, she told him that they had been cast from life and pointed out what he had missed.

In 1909 she was persuaded to write her memoirs. Called "My Recollections" they created a stir in society, afraid that some dusty old skeletons were going to be released from their closets. In the book she took revenge on Disraeli for his rejection of her by claiming that he was the pursuer, but that she could not stand his bad breath and that, upon the advice of the then Prince of Wales, had refused him. The Prince, by now Edward VII, was enraged and considered legal action but was advised against it.

The title of Earl of Cardigan had passed down through the Ailesburys and, many years ago, Adeline had overheard a conversation about Lord Robert Brudenell-Bruce, now the heir to Deene. "Bob won't have long to wait", had said the voice. There and then Adeline had resolved to outlive him. This she did successfully, Robert waiting for 44 years, dying titleless in 1912.

Adeline, Countess of Cardigan and Lancastre died on 25th May 1915, much loved by the locals despite her eccentricities. Several thousand people filed by her body as it rested in Deene church. At 91 there were few of her former lovers left to worry about their reputations, but many families were not sorry to see past indiscretions put to rest.

The past ravages of Deene Park are now slowly being put to rights and, occasionally, when the house is open to the public, seventeen rooms of the rooms are open for inspection, crammed with Brudenell history. Everywhere you look, however, there are reminders of the powerful presence of Adeline, and none more compelling than the beautiful portrait by Buckner.

Battle Of The River Nene

The battleship curved majestically through the water until she was broadside on. Slowly the gun turrets swivelled, a flash of flame, a cloud of smoke, and her opponent, the warship "Thunderer", limped away, the jagged stump of her funnel a scar of the encounter. It was just one of the engagements in the "Battle of the River Nene" that took place near Northampton's South Bridge.

Bassett Lowke, the famous local firm of model makers, had been commissioned to build a fleet of naval craft for a special display to be mounted at the Imperial Services Exhibition, at Earls Court, in 1913.

Nine ships comprised the fleet, each to be about one thirtieth the size of their real-life counterparts, and housing one or two man crews in each vessel. The larger ships were over twenty feet long and were driven by electric motors. Turrets rotated and elevated, all ships lights were operational, searchlights worked, and torpedo nets and booms could be put out.

The flotilla consisted of the Royal Yacht "Britannia", the battleship "King George V", warships "Thunderer", "Neptune", "Collosus", "New Zealand", and "Queen Mary", as well as several "enemy" ships. The models all had to be built in the ten weeks leading up to the exhibition. To facilitate the trials of the ships, and because the timber for their construction had been supplied by them, the woodsheds of Smith's Timber Company, on the banks of the river, were pressed into service as a "shipyard". Work was put into the hands of George Winteringham, Bassett Lowke's specialist model ship builder, working to designs by Edward Hobbs.

One Saturday afternoon in May 1913, the whole armada was launched near South Bridge for a trial battle. Spectators crowded the towpath and parapets, and the opportunity was seized to make a collection in aid of the Hospital Fund.

The display was to portray the battle of "Petropolis". Brock's, the firework manufacturers, were in charge of the armaments and special effects, causing the guns to fire, mines to explode, and ships to sink in flames at the appropriate times. Smoke poured from the ship's funnels as they manoeuvred to bombard "Petropolis".

The River Nene display, though only a rehearsal for the full Earls Court show, was a roaring success and was received with great enthusiasm, the mayor and mayoress of Northampton, perhaps, going a little "over the top" by making a review of the "fleet" in Mr Bassett Lowke's steam yacht "Iolanthe" after the battle.

Immediately after the engagement the model ships were loaded on railway drays for transport to Earls Court where, three times a day, they acted out the fight. Impressive though the River Nene battle was, the performance at the Imperial Services Exhibition must have been an even greater spectacle, as part of the battle depicted a night attack on the fleet, with searchlights and gunfire from "shore batteries".

One assumes that after the Exhibition the ships were broken up, for none of them are known to have survived.

Doing The Northampton Canter ....

We've all heard of the Lambeth Walk, the Boston Two-step, and Viennese Waltz, but have you ever heard of the Northampton Canter?

Just after the last war when, in every ballroom, dancers were linking arms, affecting a Cockney swagger, and shouting "Oi!" in the Lambeth Walk, Northampton was suddenly smitten by a new dance craze, the Northampton Canter.

It all began when local composer Philip Thomas got together with writer Leslie Kibble and put together the song:-

> Verse:
> There's been some talk of the Lambeth Walk,
> There's been a lot of chaff and banter,
> But I could spend
> Five hours on end
> Just doing the Northampton Canter.
> Chorus:
> You can dance as you like
> In Heckmondwike,
> You can do the Wigan Wiggle or the Huddersfield Hike
> You can waltz in Walsall if you wish,
> You can do the Plymouth Paddle or the Swansea Swish.
> For every town must have it's dance;
> They're toddling in Tidworth,
> And Preston's on the prance,
> They bound like the ballet in Biggleswade
> And wear their shoes to tatters,
> Which is good for trade.
> Variation: They talk a lot
> Of the Truro Trot
> And say that it's a regular enchanter,
> But we could spend
> A month on end
> Just doing the Northampton Canter.
> Just doing the Northampton Canter!

The lyrics are obviously written with a dance in mind, but the song's first performance was in the interlude between films at the Exchange Cinema, on the Market Square, when a number of adaptions of the tune were played on the organ by the cinema's resident musician Mr. Harold Thiems, who contrived them.

The manager of the Exchange, at this time, was Mr. M.Cowley, and he arranged for well-known Northampton dance instructor Mr. Fred Langley to devise a dance to go with the music. The dance was presented to the public for the first time on the stage of the Exchange Cinema in January of 1939 when, with the words projected on the big screen and the packed audience singing along, led by local vocalist Florence Someo, Fred Langley demonstrated the steps. Joan Austin, a young pupil of Miss Vera Pettit's Dance Academy, also entertained by tap dancing to the tune. So well received was the Northampton Canter that the original composer, Philip Thomas, was called to the stage where, in response to the acclamation of the audience, he gave a short speech finishing by hoping that Northampton "will canter to prosperity in 1939."

If you would like to try the Northampton Canter here's how to do it:-

Stand arm in arm with your partner facing down the room, lady on man's right arm. Starting with the outside foot take six steps forward. Separate and, turning inwards, tap each foot on the floor while turning to face the way you came. Repeat this manoeuvre until you are back at your starting point.

Then you take two steps forward. Both turn right taking six steps to describe a small circle in your line of dance. Immediately turn left and, in six steps, describe a similar circle, finishing in line of dance and tapping feet twice. Making, in fact, a figure of eight. Repeat this movement again.

For the third section, step forward with outside foot (one beat), lock inside foot behind it (two beats), step forward inside foot and repeat; step forward outside foot and repeat. Take six walking steps then repeat the last section, finishing with two taps. Except where stated all steps take two beats.

The music for the Northampton Canter.

Somehow I can't see this dance becoming a hit in Northampton discos, but it would be interesting to see it revived as part of local history. Perhaps a local school could recreate it as part of their social studies.

Magic .... And Tragic .... Gates

You wouldn't think, to look now at the rather ordinary gates of East Haddon Hall, that they are reminders of magic, and tragic, tales.

Now mere battered stumps, they were once ornate wrought-iron gates set upon elegant stone pillars. They were erected at the entrance to the Hall, then the home of Mr. D.C. Guthie close by the church, in 1912, and were fine examples of 17th century ironwork.

The gates as they once were. The figures have now been removed.

Originally they were made for Lord Chief Baron Sir Edward Ward, whose initials adorned the gates, and guarded the entrance to Stoke Doyle Manor House. After the distinguished judge's death the estate was inherited by a young man, Thomas Welsh Hunt, who dearly loved the view through these gates of a long avenue of trees on his Wadenhoe parkland. To make his joy complete he was to marry a clergyman's daughter, Catherine Euseby.

After the marriage the loving couple went, as was then the custom, on the Grand Tour of Europe. While honeymooning in Italy, near the small town of Paestum on the gulf of Salerno, on Friday 3rd December, 1824, their carriage was stopped by bandits, embittered gamekeepers who had been discharged from the service of the King of Naples. In the altercation one shot was fired, fatally wounding both husband and wife. He was 28 years old, she 23. They were buried at Naples.

The estate at Stoke Doyle fell into disrepair, the mansion was demolished, and the gates removed to another part of the Ward Hunt property, Berrystead at Oundle. Here they became the subject of local legend. On the top of each gatepost were ancient lead figures of the gods Apollo and Diana. Diana, the virgin huntress and goddess of the moon, faced across the gates pointing her bow and arrow at Apollo, the Greek god of sun, music and poetry, on the opposite pillar. Diana had a little dog at her feet. Local belief was that the spirits of the murdered couple now resided in the figures and that, at midnight, she would release her arrow and the dog would jump down.

In 1912 the Oundle estate was sold, but the gates were not included with the house, being sold separately. Mr Guthrie bought them for £375 and erected them at East Haddon.

Sadly, now, the gates are unhinged, the whole structure a sorry remnant of its former glory, and the gods have left their pedestals, it seems, for good.

Ridicule In Camera

A feud between a chief constable and a photographer provided some amusement for Northamptonians over one hundred years ago.

When Disderi, a Parisian photographer, invented the carte-de-visite in 1859, his intention was that these little portraits, mounted on stiff gilt-edged cards about 4" x 2½", should replace the rather boring visiting cards left by callers in the strict etiquette of the time. Soon, however, the collecting of cartes-de-visites became a craze, no Victorian parlour being complete without it's elaborately bound and clasped album. Not just family portraits were included. Stationers and photographers' shops sold vast numbers of subjects ranging from royalty, stage stars, politicians, and famous beauties, to freaks and even nudes (in the acceptable form of art poses!).

At number 13 Bridge Street, in Northampton, William Cox carried on business as a photographer. The first to advertise the carte-de-visite in town, at 1/- each, he soon faced vigorous competition, so had to reduce his price to 6d each. The fierce competition also had another effect, too, and Cox soon gained a reputation for using his camera in less savoury enterprises.

Word inevitably got back to the Chief Constable of the day, one Henry Keenan, who made vigorous and not too subtle enquiries. These were much resented by Cox who resolved to retaliate if he could.

Cox's first effort was to produce a carte-de-visite showing Keenan in his police uniform wearing, over it, the mayoral robes and chain of office, inferring that he was after the post of Northampton's first citizen. He was shown seated on a chair in the form of a cross-crowned church, alluding to his Romanism. A few lines of crude verse complete the carte, and included the phrase "Och Hone! Your Wurtships!", mocking his Irish accent. Keenan's reaction is not recorded, but he can't have been too pleased!

Then, in July 1874, Keenan found himself in the midst of a bitter local controversy, and Cox joined the fray with glee. A family of eight died in a spectacular firework explosion in a house on the Mounts.

The incident occurred on the night of Tuesday, 20th July, 1874. Police Sergeant Smith was patrolling the Mounts when the street was illuminated by two brilliant flashes. Lightning, he thought, until, without warning, a huge column of flame erupted from the three storey house of number 45, where lived a plasterer, Mr. Benjamin Smith, his wife and six children.

As a spare-time occupation, for the last ten years, Smith had made fireworks for fetes and carnivals, having learned his craft while travelling with one of the country's leading pyrotechnicians.

That fateful Tuesday, he had just completed an order for £40 worth of fireworks for Newport Pagnell Horticultural Fete. He worked, so his neighbours said, in the lower floor kitchen where there was usually a large fire upon which Mrs. Smith cooked for her brood, and where the family lived.

No-one knows how the fireworks ignited, but the results were horrifying. Not only did the fireworks go off, but a large stock of ingredients burnt, too. Molten brimstone flowed down the stairs, rockets shot in all directions, coloured fire blazed from the windows, and rescuers were showered with multicoloured sparks.

First on the scene were Sergeant Smith and Mr. George Green of the Volunteer Fire Brigade, both of whom made brave attempts to enter the building. As they burst open the front door of the house, Mr Smith staggered out wearing only his shirt. His hair and clothes were alight and he was dreadfully burned. Two boys, William, aged 16 and Henry, 14, were at an upstairs window crying in terror. Neighbours implored them to jump, William landing on the pavement, and Henry being caught by a Mr Hough. Police Sergeant Smith, meanwhile, had gathered a pile of bedding and clothes to form a cushion into which, it was hoped, survivors could leap.

The eleven year old daughter Louisa appeared at a window but was afraid to jump. She hung on until, eventually, she was so badly burned that she fell. Mrs. Smith, meanwhile, had been trying to save her youngest child, four month old Frank, and she had reached a back window. She got out of the window and held on while neighbours tried to raise a plank to form a slide to safety. The fire, however, forced her to let go, the baby being found beneath the body of the injured mother in the garden.

By now two fire brigades had arrived on the scene, the Volunteer Brigade and the Town Brigade, but there was little that they could do but control the blaze. The intensity of the fire was such that from the time of the first flash to the extinction of the fire, a mere three quarters of an hour had elapsed. The building had to be demolished, as the initial explosions had forced joists out of the walls. Work was made even more dangerous by canisters of unexploded chemicals which, miraculously, had not ignited.

In the ruins were found the remaining two children, Sarah Ann aged 17, and Kate aged 4, their bodies practically unidentifiable having fallen through the entire house from bedroom to cellar.

The death toll, at the end of it all, was eight. Benjamin Smith, his wife Ann, and their whole family of six children.

The firework factory was plainly illegal, but nevertheless was well-known throughout the town, having been in operation for some years. Searching questions were asked, and strong criticism voiced in the press, of the Chief Constable. How was it that everyone in the town, it seemed, knew of this firework arsenal except, apparently, Keenan? Did he turn a blind eye? Was he even bribed?

Then, to add fuel to the controversy, there appeared a carte-de-visite cartoon from Cox. It showed the head of the Chief Constable as the body of a six-tailed comet, the tail of which has ignited the Mounts house. There was, in fact, a comet visible in the sky at about this time and one of the common theories was that, somehow, this had sparked off the explosion. Beneath the picture were the lines:- "Who caused the explosions on the Mounts? Was it the Six-Tailed Comet, or the Chief of Bluelight? What's that to me, or any other man, eh? BUT WHO'S TO BLAME?" The last but one line was the refrain of a song popular in Northampton at the time.

It is not clear whether Keenan had words with Cox about these photographic enterprises, or how the skirmishing was resolved, but Keenan certainly seems to fade from public view thenceforth.

The cartoon carte-de-visite bearing the head of the chief constable.

The King's Artificial Limb ....

You didn't know that the King had an artificial limb? Neither did the men attending to him way back in 1928, but if you look at him closely you can observe it for yourself.

I am talking, of course, about King Charles II who, incongruously clad in Roman clothing and full-bottomed wig, is portrayed in stone above the portico of All Saints Church, in the centre of Northampton.

Over sixty years ago it was discovered that the original oak beams of the portico, a gift of the King from the forests of Whittlebury and Salcey after the church had been destroyed in the Great Fire of 1675, were riddled with dry rot and were unsafe. The beams were replaced with steel girders under the direction of architect Colonel John Brown. Just to be on the safe side, the rest of the structure was closely examined at the same time. Whilst the body of the church was in fine fettle, one surprising thing was discovered. King Charles had a wooden arm!

A workman, cleaning the statue with a wire brush, revealed that the King's arm, holding a baton, was carved from mahogany and cunningly painted to resemble the pale stone of the rest of the figure. This had never been noted before, and it was certainly never recorded in the many histories of the church that had been written over the years.

Then, an anonymous old man visited the church and, talking to the vicar, the Rev. J.T. Lewis, admitted that he was to blame. Thirty years previously the man had been engaged on similar restoration work when he accidentally snapped off the arm, which fell and broke into many fragments. As it was plainly irreparable, he had a friendly carpenter carve a replica in wood. This he skilfully grafted on to the statue, painting it so cunningly that it had remained undetected for thirty years.

Now the original paint has long disappeared and the wood weathered to a dark colour. Recent restoration has blended the arm into the rest of the figure once again and it may be that a replacement stone arm will be sculpted. The wooden limb is, by now, a part of history and, one might say, an unusual monument to the many craftsmen who have worked on the church these last three hundred years, so it would, I think, be a shame to see it go.

How Paddy's Meadow Got Its Name

"How did Paddy's Meadow get it's name?", someone asked the other day. Paddy's Meadow, for any Northamptonians that do not know, is the grass wedge that squeezes itself between Spencer Bridge Road, St. Andrew's Road and the River Nene just across the road, in fact, from the Super Sausage cafe and lorry park if you are a young person, or the Slipper Baths and Miller's Meadow if you are of an older generation.

Years ago, before the river was allowed to silt itself up, it ran clean and deep through the meadows of Semilong. Indeed, otters were frequently observed as far downstream as Spencer Bridge, and the river was a favourite bathing place for the local children. To cater for the hordes of swimmers that gathered there, crude facilities were soon erected; primitive changing huts and a few rickety sheds.

"Keeper" of this bathing place, unofficial lifeguard, and self-appointed swimming teacher to masses of kids from the "boroughs", who could afford very little else in the way of sports facilities, was one Patrick Moore, an Irishman known to one and all as "Paddy".

Paddy had served in the army in the days when discipline was harsh, and he brought some of this regime into the lives of many of the urchins who flocked around him, and he was loved for it. His customary attire was a thick suit with a waistcoat, a short "swagger" cane and a battered straw hat that was swapped on Sundays for an only slightly less tattered panama. Beneath the hat a heavily tanned face with bristling military moustache and mischievously twinkling eyes.

He made this bathing place his home and, in the summer, ruled it strictly from dawn to dusk. Often he could be seen surrounded by a crowd of naked boys, for most children bathed nude in those days, all seated on the grass while Paddy instructed them in swimming and diving. He was not averse, either, to recounting tall tales of his travels with the Colours. The cane that he carried could be put to good use, too. At the end of the day his cry was, "A prize for the last boy out ......", this prize being a whack from Paddy's cane!

Such was the demand for the baths that Paddy decreed that bathers were only allowed in the river once a day, and he had a hawk-like eye and a retentive memory, and woe betide any child trying to get two swims in one day. The shrill whistle emitted by the use of two fingers and mouth by Paddy was enough to send urchins scurrying.

When the bathing place was first opened the gathering of scruffy kids obviously worried the police, who paid a few visits, but it soon became clear that Paddy had the situation well under control, and thenceforth, the sight of a "Bobby" was rare indeed in the meadow.

Grown-ups, too, used the bathing place and Paddy formed many friendships with figures of note, all of whom he shamelessly exploited for the benefit of "his boys." Thus Lord Lewis would attend with a friend and throw shillings and half-crowns into the river for the lads to dive for. As this was in the days before the river bed was concreted into a regular pool, the coins sank into the muddy bottom and had to be searched for. Tom Douglas an amateur boxing champion, Alderman Hannen, and Mr. Thurston Shoosmith were also habitués, Mr. Shoosmith, a solicitor, giving up a lot of his own time in teaching youngsters to swim.

Paddy's teaching style was distinctly military. He would line the children up as though on parade and number them off.....1,2,3,etc, sometimes up to 40 before despatching them into the water under his eagle eye.

Over the years the bathing place became much worn with constant use and so was tidied up by the construction of a concrete basin.

Paddy, however, still ruled his empire from his little wooden hut on the bank, where he kept as pets several birds and dogs. Very privileged adults were received into this holy of holies, where they had their "arms twisted" to provide prizes for the sports days that Paddy had started to organise for local lads. A great supporter was William Page, "Uncle Bill" to the boys, a pawnbroker from Scarletwell Street, who supplied medals and prizes from his own pocket.

Eventually, when old age and infirmity caught up with Paddy, the Corporation found him a niche as a street sweeper. The old man was almost broken-hearted at having to leave his beloved "baths" and his earnings were often supplemented by surreptitious tips from "old boys" that he had taught to swim. After this he did not live long and passed over, mourned by many "borough" boys.

The bathing place at Paddy's Meadow slowly became weed-logged and silted, the structure fell into decay, and in 1938 was closed down. The mouldering remains fell apart and were vandalised until, eventually, the entire area was cleared, landscaped, and seeded to make the pleasant walkway that it is today.

Patrick Moore, that benign dictator of the baths, has his epitaph in the name Paddy's Meadow, and I have a feeling that he would be very proud of that ......

Parachute Joe

Northamptonshire's past seems to have been dotted with some extraordinary characters. Whether today's way of life obliterates individuality, or whether we are now too busy to notice life's quirks, is debatable, but there is no doubt that life would be richer with a few more eccentrics around.

Wiser than they gave him credit for, at the time, was "Parachute Joe". Joe Ingram was born in 1850, a native of Harrowden, though he lived variously at Burton Latimer, Finedon and Wellingborough, and was, by profession, a steeplejack. He was a familiar sight around the county as he fearlessly climbed church spires and chimneys doing essential repair work. What marked him out from other such workmen, was that he had a habit of demonstrating his courage by performing some breath-taking feat of balance at the summit.

On one memorable occasion he climbed the spire of Kettering parish church by way of the crockets, the curled foliage projections, and stood aloft on the weather-vane waving his handkerchief to spectators. He similarly climbed Rushden and Bozeat spires, and, at the age of 69, to celebrate the end of World War I, ascended the steeple of Wellingborough church to attach a flag to the top.

Joe, however, had a dream. That aeroplanes would, one day, revolutionise travel. His first experiments were with parachutes and were probably prompted by the idea of making a safe landing should he fall from a spire. Soon he was making models of various designs of parachute and launching them from church towers. He then approached the vicar of St. Mary's Church, in Kettering, for permission to launch himself from the spire to test a full-sized canopy, but was refused.

On one occasion, in 1888, he built a 40 feet high scaffolding tower on the Victoria Grounds and proposed to launch himself from the top using a canvas tilt, such as was used for covering railway wagons, as a parachute. The Deputy Chief Constable of Wellingborough, Superintendent Baillee, forbade him to attempt it. Ingram, therefore, demonstrated his 'chute with a man-sized weight attached, the distance which it penetrated into the ground leaving no doubt that the experiment would have been fatal.

He offered to give an exhibition of his parachutes at Lord George Sanger's Circus and, in his proposals, described himself as "Teitan, Prince of the Air". The circus turned him down.

By 1911 he had moved on to the construction of model aeroplanes, which he tested around his home town. Many were claimed to fly successfully. The arrival in the county, that year, of the Daily Mail £10,000 air race gave Joe a chance to air his views on aviation. "Aeroplanes will eventually be built", he said, "which will carry a hundred people. They will make present day machines as obsolete as the stagecoach".

A contemporary photograph shows Joe's model aeroplane to be a rather kite-like device, but with horizontally rotating fans, or rotors, operating somewhat like a helicopter. The power source is not discernable, but the machine looks practical as a glider, even if it

Parachute Joe Ingram with one of his model aircraft.

would not climb vertically.

In a sarcastically worded article in a local newspaper, a reporter, with obviously less vision or imagination than Parachute Joe, poured ridicule on the inventor, especially since Joe had asked to be allowed to fly with local aviation pioneer Will Moorhouse and to jump by parachute from his plane.

Joe Ingram was obviously a man of considerable determination, for he was also a road walker and pedestrian racer of some note, though in his middle years, and he persevered with his aerial experiments despite being cruelly taunted as a crackpot.

During World War I he bombarded the naval and the military authorities with ideas and inventions relating to aerial warfare, some of which now seem remarkably advanced. In 1916 he proposed an aircraft weighing 25 tons and capable of lifting ten tons of guns, ammunition and bombs, as well as twenty men. Shaped, as he described it, "somewhat like a submarine", i.e. streamlined, it would fly at 300 mph. He planned that it would be propelled by 2,000 horse power engines that worked on the principal of vacuum in one part and compressed gas in another, and that is the theory behind jet propulsion.

Though many of his notions eventually came to pass, he was given no credit for his foresight.

Parachute Joe eventually died in Northampton Workhouse at the age of 72, in the early days of the New Year of 1922. He lived to see giant aircraft deliver devastating bomb-loads, the crossing of the Atlantic, the first all-metal aeroplanes, and the carrying of parachutes on all military aircraft, all of which he had forecast.

Coincidentally, the year of his death also saw the invention, by Juan de la Cierva, of the variable pitch rotor, the one thing that made helicopters practical ..... in view of his model designs, how Joe would have loved that!

The Galloping Ghost Of Sywell

There is not much traffic using Church Lane, Sywell, but if, in the quiet of the night of the first Wednesday in June, you hear the sound of horses hoofs, stand back and await the passing of Sywell's galloping ghost.

The apparition is the spectre of racehorse Maccabeus who met his end close by, in the summer of 1844.

One of the favoured entries in that year's Derby at Epsom was Running Rein, owned by a Mr. A. Wood. The horse won handsomely, and profitably, at odds of 10 to 1. The Derby, of course, is for three year olds, and there was evidently some suspicion that Running Rein's declaration was inaccurate. Word was that this was not Running Rein, but a more experienced horse disguised to look like it. Accordingly, Lord George Bentinck, of the Jockey Club, and Lords Glasgow and Maidstone, lodged objections. The owner of the second finishing horse Orlando, a Colonel Peel, was not too happy either and joined the clamour, claiming the £4,250 stake, withheld by the stewards, as his.

Colonel Peel was told that the onus of proving his claim that Running Rein was a ringer, a substitute horse, was upon him, if he wanted the horse disqualified.

Meanwhile, Running Rein had been returned to its stables at Sywell House, where the growing rumpus in racing circles was creating quite a panic. It seemed likely that Running Rein would have to be produced so that its age and identity could be established.

The Running Rein that was first past the post was, in fact, really a horse called Maccabeus and was a four year old. The whole matter was rapidly coming to a head so, at dead of night, poor Maccabeus, alias Running Rein, was slaughtered and buried in the grounds of Sywell House. The animal's head was cut off and a three year old horse's head buried with the body, just in case an exhumation should be ordered.

As the accusations could not be satisfactorily answered by the owner, Colonel Peel's objection was upheld and Orlando proclaimed the winner of the 1844 Derby. Mr. Wood and his advisors were warned off from racing and the whole matter faded into the mists of time. Or it would have if, as local people swear, Maccabeus's ghost did not leave the grave and make its ghostly gallop down the lane every Derby Day at dead of night.

The Decline And Fall Of Northampton's Castle

Mists lay thick across the meadows of the River Nene. Out of the grey blanket rose the forbidding fortifications of the castle, its gloomy outline broken, at parapet and porte, by the glint of arms and armour. Getting nearer is the jingling sound of harness and the clop of hoofs, mingled with the heavy rumble of wagon wheels. Suddenly, from the fog, erupts all the pomp and panoply of a Royal Progress. Colourfully caparisoned horses, richly cloaked courtiers, and guards with arms gleaming are followed by a heavy baggage train and all the trappings of a regal household on the move. The King has arrived at Northampton Castle.

It is a scene which must have been repeated many times in the history of the castle, for its importance as a royal residence for the Normans and the Plantagenets spanned several centuries. The great mound in the loop of the river to the west of Northampton was a natural defensive position and the first real castle on the site was erected by Simon de St. Liz, the first Earl of Northampton, who came to England during the reign of William the Conqueror's son, William Rufus. After marrying the king's cousin Matilda he founded the Priory of St. Andrew in the town about 1094 and rebuilt much of the town, which was in ruins, and constructed a defensive wall all around it. Soon after, he went off to the Holy Land with the first Crusade and, after taking part in the capture of Jerusalem, returned home and, in thanksgiving, built the Church of the Holy Sepulchre. His experiences ensured that his Northampton castle was almost impregnable.

The first royal presence at the castle is noted in 1106, when King Henry I who was at war with his brother Robert, Duke of Normandy, parleyed here to no avail. The Duke returned to France in high dudgeon, but was taken prisoner and spent the next 28 years in captivity. The castle came into royal possession about the time of Simon de St. Liz's death on the way home from yet another Crusade. Exactly how the King acquired it is not known, but he must have liked the place for in 1122 he is said to have spent Easter here in great state. He evidently was busy extending the castle area, too, for eight years later he paid the powerful monks at the nearby St. Andrew's Priory 3/8d as recompense for lands which he had enclosed.

The castle must have been a formidable structure, at this time, for it was surrounded on three sides by a defensive ditch, or foss, some 90 feet wide and around 30 feet deep.

Added to this was a bank another 80 feet wide and 20 feet to its top making, in effect a 50 foot obstacle. The southwest side was protected by the loop of the river. Thick walls surrounded the area, punctuated by towers. The entrance to the castle was on the north side where there was a gate and a barbican. The great hall, on the ground floor, was capable of being reached on horseback, and the royal quarters had two chambers, one above another. All in all, the castle enclosed an oval area nearly 500 feet by 350 feet.

Certainly, the nobles who were summoned here to a parliament in 1131 and pressed to renew their oath of fealty to the king's daughter Maud, the empress, affirming her as heir to the throne, must have felt the power of the place. The king's weakly son had died and he needed to consolidate his daughter's position. In the castle's great hall the knights and barons bent their knee and swore allegiance to her, albeit with tongue in cheek, for four years later, upon Henry's death, not Maud, but the king's nephew Stephen, Count of Blois, was made king.

In 1138 King Stephen, the last of the Norman kings, was at Northampton castle receiving in Council all bishops, abbots, barons and knights of the land, a concourse that must have taxed the castle, and the town's, limited accommodation to the utmost. How often he visited is vague, but 1142 sees Stephen back at the castle and sick. Unable to travel he stayed here from April to June. Keeping the powerful and predatory barons at bay was a feat for any king of that time, and in 1146 Stephen survived a devious plot against him by Ranulph, the Earl of Chester, whilst staying at Northampton. The earl came to the King with a small band of followers to beg for the monarchs assistance in controlling the Welsh, who were making incursions into the borderlands. He, praising the King's bravery, claimed that only his personal presence at the head of an army would ensure the defeat of the Welsh. The King, flattered, agreed. As they discussed the tactics the earl became more and more agitated and concerned that they should set forth in haste. The king's councillors, noticing this, became suspicious and investigated, only to find that an armed group awaited ready to murder Stephen. Chester was accused of conspiring with the Duke of Normandy against the King and thrown into the castle's dungeons, where he was held until he bought his freedom by surrendering Lincoln Castle and several other properties to the Crown as security for his future loyalty.

Henry II, the first of the Plantagenet kings, ascended the throne in 1154 and very soon we see him, too, at Northampton Castle, sorting out a row between quarrelling clergy. The Abbot Silvester of St. Augustines, Canterbury refused to profess to Archbishop Theobald and the king called a council ordering the abbott to do so. This he refused to do until a letter was received from the Pope ordering him to comply. The religious turmoil among the clergy came to a head in 1164 when the king decided that clergy accused of offences should appear before lay tribunals, rather than be tried before their peers.

Thomas Becket, Archbishop of Canterbury, refused to agree and was ordered to appear at Northampton Castle before a council of the states. He stayed at St. Andrews Priory and had several meetings with the King at the castle. At one a note of farce was introduced by the monarch retreating to an upstairs chamber whilst Becket remained below, the furious argument being maintained by a flock of monks rushing up and down stairs to transmit each point. At their final meeting, although this was not strictly a trial, Robert, Earl of Leicester, started talking of a "judgement", and Becket, being advised by his supporters that he was at risk, withdrew, mounted his horse and with his friend Herbert of Bosham up behind, went to the Priory between cheering townsfolk and clergy. That night, in teeming rain, disguised as a monk with the name of Dereman, he left by the town's North Gate for Flanders. At Canterbury he was surprised in the cathedral and murdered before the altar. The King was consumed by guilt of this crime for the rest of his life, despite twice being absolved of blame by Papal legates.

As well as the continuing problems with the church, Henry now had trouble with his barons. In the May of 1174 rebel barons attacked Northampton Castle killing or wounding some 200 men and capturing another 200, all of whom were marched off as prisoners to Leicester. Henry, who was in France, returned in July and, after stopping at Canterbury Cathedral to do penance for Becket's death, arrived at Northampton.

William the Lion, King of Scotland, who had sided with the barons, had been captured at Alnwick, and was brought to Northampton where he entered the town tied under the belly of a horse. Five days later the rebellious noblemen and clergy surrendered the castles that had stood against the king and made submission to him.

Conflicts in France continued to plague Henry II but the Christmas of 1176 saw him again at Northampton Castle, with his sons Geoffrey and John. Whether it was a peaceful festival or not we can only guess, but a council was called for the 13th January so that the Count of Flanders could beg the hand of Henry's two nieces for his son and nephew.

The cost of upkeep of the castle about this time can be gained from some of the items of expenditure. For the King's maintenance at Northampton for four days £32. 6s. 5d. To garrison ten men-at-arms in the castle for 306 days from Michaelmas to 1st August cost £153 in wages whilst 118 men-at-arms who were under the charge of the castle's constable for 20 days were paid £118 in all. Ordinary soldiers, when taken on got a small lump sum (the equivalent of the later "King's shilling", perhaps) and 8d a day for the first 35 days, and 1/- a day from then onwards, food being provided.

Henry II seemed to find Northampton a convenient centre of government and 1179 finds him at the castle calling a convention of prelates and barons to confirm and reinforce a review of the system of dispensing justice. The country was to be divided up into six judicial circuits and three judges were appointed to travel throughout each area. To this council, by royal command, came the King of Scotland to swear loyalty to the Church of England.

Upon Henry's death, Richard I, the Lionheart, came to the throne and, before a year had passed was involved, like his predecessors, in another ecclesiastical wrangle. While the king was absent in the Holy Land, on a Crusade, a squabble broke out between Prince John and Longchamp, Bishop of Ely, the chancellor, over custody of castles in the Kingdom, including that at Northampton. The matter was settled, eventually, with the mediation of the bishops and custody was given to Simon de Pateshull as constable, who agreed that if the King died without issue, he would deliver up the castle to John.

Richard, after his spell of captivity in Germany, was in need of recuperation when he returned to England in 1194. What place better than Northampton Castle, where he arrived on Easter Eve? Peace and quiet was not what he got, however, for William of

Scotland, who was attending the King here, was laying claim to the border counties. Richard's problem was that if he refused William it would upset the delicate diplomatic negotiations to settle the French wars, while, if he gave William Northumberland etc, it would be seen as his fear of the Scottish/French alliance. He arrived at a compromise and issued a charter from Northampton; the counties were to remain English, but William and his heirs, whenever summoned to the king's councils in England, should be met at the border by the sheriff and escorted across each county by successive sheriffs. Whilst in England, William's expenses were to be defrayed by the Crown.

Simon de Pateshull remained as constable of Northampton Castle, and sheriff of the county for nine years and saw the throne pass, on Richard's death at the age of 42, to John, who as king, made him Chief Justice of Common Pleas. King John, in his 17 year reign, came to Northampton Castle 30 times. As a base it was ideally situated, and about 1208 he moved his treasury to Northampton, probably at the Castle. During one of his stays his accounts list payments of 6/8d for bringing his personal hunting gear from London and 28/6d for a carriage and harness for the Queen. More darkly, there is also payment of 6/- to sergeants at arms who brought in the heads of six outlaws. On one occasion, too, he fed 1000 poor folk of the town at a cost to himself of £5. 14s. 7d.

John, like earlier kings, was having trouble with the clergy and, in 1211, he met two Papal legates at the castle, one a Knight Templar. They came to induce the king to cease his persecution of the church and threatened to excommunicate him. The Pope had nominated one Stephen as Archbishop of Canterbury, while the King had named his own man. King John's reply was that "If Stephen sets foot in the Kingdom I will have him hanged". He then offered, if Stephen was to withdraw from Canterbury, to give him another see and appoint any other of the Pope's nominees to the archbishopric of Canterbury. The Pope's representatives saw this as a loss of face, and said "No". In a rage, and in an attempt to intimidate the legates, the King ordered a group of prisoners brought into the Great Hall, all convicted criminals. In view of the clergy some were hanged, others eyes were put out, some had hands or feet cut off. Finally, a fraudulent clerk was brought in and ordered to be hanged. Goaded beyond endurance, one of the legates went to make preparations for the ceremony of excommunication. Realising that he had gone too far, the King sent after him and handed over the clerk for trial by the church. The matter dragged on for nearly two years before the King was forced to back down.

The barons, who were still fermenting unrest, banded together to demand restoration of rights granted to them in a charter by Henry I and, in 1215, marched on Northampton Castle. Under the command of Robert Fitzwalter "Marshal of the Army of God and the Holy Church", they laid siege to the castle for 14 days. So strong were the fortifications that they were unable to take it, as they had arrived without battering rams or siege engines. Upon the death of Fitzwalter, shot by a crossbow bolt from the castle walls, the attackers retired. Where an army failed, though, the townspeople of Northampton succeeded. A few weeks later men of the town attacked the royal garrison at the castle and killed a good number of them. The soldiers retaliated by burning much of Northampton.

King John, however, could read the signs and on 15th June 1215, at Runnymede, signed the Magna Carta. He surrendered four important castles, including that at

Northampton, which was handed over to Roger de Nevill, as governor, together with lands and tithes at Kingsthorpe sufficient for its upkeep.

Peace did not last long, and three months later the King was again holding the castle, and the barons were again attacking it, but this time with the appropriate siege engines. King John, however, returned in the nick of time to repel the offensive.

As the 13th Century progressed the pattern persisted. The throne passed, in 1216, to Henry III, John's devout and godly son, plagued, like his father, with rebellious barons. Fulk de Breaut, a Norman soldier with an evil reputation, was appointed as Northampton Castle's constable. For the Christmas of that year Breaut played host to the king at the castle and paid all expenses. Just a few years later, Henry again spent Christmas here and as an amnesty, freed at the special request of the royal physician Roger Lacoc, one Ralph de Eyneston who had been imprisoned in the castle for leading three greyhounds through the Royal Forest without leashes.

From Northampton Castle, Fulk de Breaut sent troops far and wide to pillage, plunder, and seize lands. His brother William was governor of Bedford Castle, and had seized Henry de Braybrok and other judges, holding them in dungeons at Bedford. Henry was outraged, summoned his supporters and marched on Bedford. It is illuminating that the king got to Newport Pagnell, on this punitive expedition, before he discovered that he had left his wine behind, and promptly sent word to the sheriff of Northampton to send 4 casks of his special wine on without delay! After two months siege, Bedford Castle was taken, the fortress destroyed, and William Breaut with 80 of the garrison hanged. Fulk fled to Wales, but finding no sanctuary, was forced to return to Northampton Castle and throw himself on the King's mercy. His life was spared, though he was expelled from the realm.

Henry III, like most medieval kings, was short of money and in 1226 demanded that Northampton should pay 1200 marks in aid, on top of the standing levy of 1/15th of transactions in the town. Other injustices roused the barons to anger, too, notably the cancellation of the charter of forests, removing many rights of the nobles. They rebelled and a council was summoned at Northampton Castle at which agreement was reached.

It was not all warfare and intrigue at the castle, however. As well as the usual court banquets and carousing, there were jousts and tournaments. In 1239 Henry organised a tourney in honour of the Queen's uncle, Peter de Savoy, who was visiting England. The lists were to be England versus Savoyards. Unwisely, the king backed the foreigners, thus inferring that he had little confidence in his own knights! Intended as a trial of skill, the whole event took a nasty turn, violence was threatened, and the tourney looked like getting out of hand. The king perceived the danger just in time and cancelled the lists.

Another joust was organised at the castle eight years later, but Henry, perhaps remembering the earlier one, sent orders to stop it. Two years later it was proposed to hold yet another tournament on 19th February 1249, and this time the knights vowed to go ahead and fight whatever the king said. In the event, the clash did not occur, for weather stopped play ...... it snowed!

Northampton Castle was the favourite residence of Henry III and various improvements to the castle were put in hand in following years. Many of the old wall openings were being glazed and windows inserted. The sheriff was told to have white glass installed in the

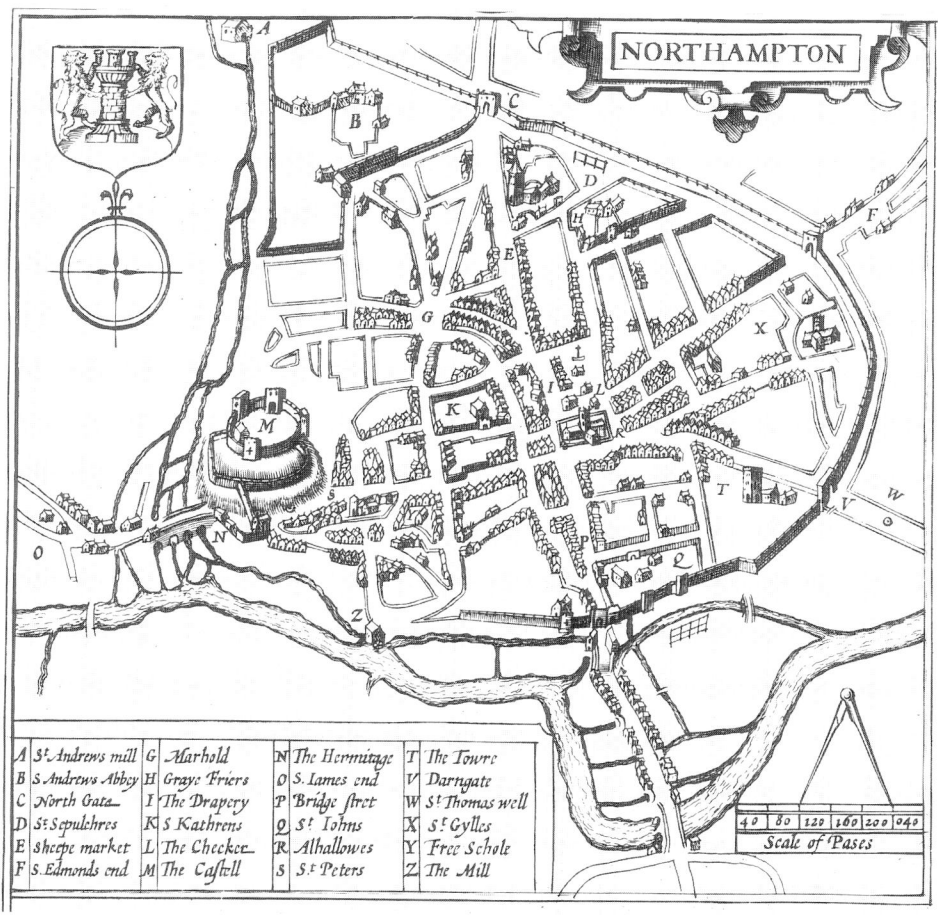

The Castle, as it was shown on Speed's famous 17th century map.

Queen's chamber and in the chapels, one in the keep and one in the castle body. One set was to be painted with the story of Dives and Lazarus.

Nearing the end of Henry III's reign the barons once more were in conflict with the king and Northampton Castle was held by the confederated barons, with Simon de Montford the younger as its governor on their behalf. The king laid siege to the town and called the defenders to parley in the fields of Cow Meadow. Meanwhile, on the north side of the town the monks of St Andrews Priory had opened up the town walls through their gardens and admitted 40 horsemen. With the town captured, Simon was arrested but spared on his oath of allegiance. Many of Northampton's defenders in this insurrection were Oxford students who had fought with slings and bows under their own college banners. The king threatened to hang them all, but relented, forbidding all scholars, from that time on, to reside in Northampton.

Edward I, likewise, found Northampton a useful base for his travels and, in 1290 we find him at the castle entertaining the town's various religious establishments, the Blackfriars, the Greyfriars and the Whitefriars ...... but each on separate days. Christmas was celebrated here by the king and his Queen, Margaret..

Less happily, the castle was being used as a prison at this time, with Welsh and Scottish prisoners secured here. Edward's death, in 1307, brought the court to Northampton again, this time to arrange the state funeral and to discuss the coronation of Edward II and the state of the nation. Criminals convicted by the courts were incarcerated in the dungeons, men like Adam Clypstone who, in 1304, had robbed the parson at Clipston and set fire to his house.

The crown of Edward II was unstable and for this reason tourneys gave nobles a chance to meet and plot. In 1313, before the king left Northampton he left orders that no tournaments should be held while he was away. He was right to be careful, for a few years later, while he was here, John Poydras, a tanner's son from Exeter, appeared at the castle during the July parliament claiming to be the real son of Edward I and that Edward II was a substitute. He was condemned as a madman and an impostor, dragged through the town and executed in public on 20th July.

Part of the castle was destroyed that same year by fire, an ever-present danger in the close-built confines of the fortress, the lower chapel and six small houses within the walls falling down. Part of the structure was still unusable after a similar fire during Edward I's time.

Edward II was deposed in 1327 in favour of Edward III. He was more in favour of tourneys and jousts and, in 1342 organised lists at Northampton Castle over Easter. It gave the knights a chance to settle a few scores, it seems, for John de Beauchamp was killed and many nobles severely injured. A number were mutilated and lots of valuable horses killed.

The custody of the castle was still the subject of controversy and was claimed by Thomas Wake, the then sheriff, as being annexed to the County and thus under his jurisdiction. An inquisition in 1329 agreed with him and ordered the crown to surrender it to the sheriff and his successors. After centuries of governments from the castle, the last parliament was held here in 1380, in the reign of Richard II. Two interesting occurrences marked the 33 day long deliberations. John Kirkeby, who had led a treasonable insurrection in London and had murdered the Genoese envoy, was brought to the castle and tried. At the same time Ralph de Ferrers and Sir Thomas, the parson at Great Brington, were tried for writing treasonable correspondence with the King of France. It was found that the missives had been forged by a mendicant friar who had then denounced the two men. Both were freed and the friar imprisoned in their stead.

Also, and topically as it happens, poll tax was introduced here. Tax had to be paid at the rate of 6/8d from each priest or monk and 1/- from every man

A model reconstruction of Northampton Castle part of an exhibit in Northampton's Central Museum, Guildhall Road.

and woman. The act set in motion the rebellions of Wat Tyler and Jack Straw.

Without the royal favour the castle now started to fall into neglect. In 1443 we find John Badle in charge as porter and gaoler, a large section being used as a prison. A century later no part of the castle was fit for habitation by King Henry VIII when he stopped in the town on his way to York. He and his entourage slept at the house of Mr. Humfrie just outside the south gate of the town.

Elizabeth's reign came and went with the castle getting more and more dilapidated, so that by Charles I's time grazing was possible within the walls. The lease for custody of the castle, the meadows within the custodianship, herbage outside and within the moat, the meadow and fishery, were assigned to the Earl of Warwick and Sir John Coke.

As the Civil War broke out it was felt judicious to maintain a Commonwealth garrison at the castle. In 1642, after an attack by Royalist horse, 60 prisoners were held in the castle and, likewise after the disastrous Battle of Naseby, the castle was again used to hold Royalist prisoners, so many being taken that the overflow was put into churches and halls in the town. The town itself was a Puritan stronghold and, upon the restoration of the monarchy an order was made by the King and Council, signed on 30th June 1662, for the "slighting of the town" and the demolition of the walls, gates and most of the castle. The Lord Lieutenants of the county, the Earls of Westmoreland and Exeter, were charged with the work and they went about it with a will. Just two weeks later, with the levelling well under way, they had to release most of the local labourers for the harvest. With the king's permission, leave was given to anyone to come and take stone from the site, free to whoever removed it. Thus it came about that several buildings within the town were made from the castle stones, one such being the outhouses of the Plough Inn.

The Postern Gate, once the back entrance, or private gate, to the castle, as it now stands on Black Lion Hill. This is the only portion of the fortress to survive.

Only enough of the castle yard was to be left so as to provide shelter for the justices, who still met here, and the site sold to Robert Haselrig. All arms within the castle were to be taken and laid up securely in the town for the defence of the realm. The walls surrounding the town were torn down at the same time to prevent them ever standing against the crown again.

From then on most mention of Northampton Castle relates to trials. Two courts of justice were established here and a sizeable gaol. In 1665 many Quakers came before the Justices at the castle and were given seven years transportation to Barbados. The towns administrators, however, had a rooted dislike of running their town from within the royal walls, and determined to have their own meeting place. Accordingly, in 1670, the Assizes were finally removed from the castle to a wooden shed built for the purpose on the Market Square. Again the castle was plundered for materials.

The situation was left with the Corporation in the town and the County in the castle. The Haselrig family, who had bought the castle at the Restoration tried to sell it in 1730, when Sir Arthur offered the castle, orchards, kennels for hounds, and his Marefair house for sale, but with little result. By 1860 the castle was said to have been quite destroyed, very little remaining, and was still up for sale.

The final part was offered on the market on 19th June, 1861 and bought by Samuel Walker. His purpose was revealed soon after when he started excavations on the site with the intention of finding treasure .....!!

The expansion of the railways and the need to establish marshalling yards near to the station caused the London, North Western Railway to buy the castle site from William Walker, on 18th December 1876, the plan being to tear down the surviving walls and to level the castle mound. The townsfolk immediately organised a petition to press for the preservation of part of the structure. The only concession was the removal and reconstruction of the old postern gate near to Black Lion Hill. In 1879 the destruction began and, by the end of the year was complete ...... nothing remained of the once impregnable Northampton Castle.